Guiding Your Teenager with Special
Needs through the Transition
from School to Adult Life

of related interest

Building a Joyful Life with your Child who has Special Needs
Nancy J. Whiteman and Linda Roan-Yager
ISBN 978 1 84310 841 2

Realizing the College Dream with Autism or Asperger Syndrome
A Parent's Guide to Student Success
Ann Palmer
ISBN 978 1 84310 801 6

Speaking Up
A Plain Text Guide to Advocacy 4-volume set
John Tufail and Kate Lyon
(Set) ISBN 978 1 84310 474 2

Talking Teenagers
Information and Inspiration for Parents of Teenagers
with Autism or Asperger's Syndrome
Ann Boushéy
ISBN 978 1 84310 844 3

The Complete Guide to Asperger's Syndrome
Tony Attwood
ISBN 978 1 84310 495 7

Kids in the Syndrome Mix of ADHD, LD, Asperger's, Tourette's, Bipolar, and More!
The one stop guide for parents, teachers, and other professionals
Martin L. Kutscher MD
With a contribution from Tony Attwood
With a contribution from Robert R Wolff MD
ISBN 978 1 84310 810 8 Hardback
ISBN 978 1 84310 811 5 Paperback

How to Find Work that Works for People with Asperger Syndrome
The Ultimate Guide for Getting People with Asperger Syndrome into the
Workplace (and keeping them there!)
Gail Hawkins
ISBN 978 1 84310 151 2

Asperger's Syndrome and Sexuality
From Adolescence through Adulthood
Isabelle Hénault
Foreword by Tony Attwood
ISBN 978 1 84310 189 5

Friendships
The Aspie Way
Wendy Lawson
Foreword by Emma Wall
ISBN 978 1 84310 427 8

Guiding Your Teenager with Special Needs through the Transition from School to Adult Life

Tools for Parents

Mary Korpi

Jessica Kingsley Publishers
London and Philadelphia

First published in 2008
by Jessica Kingsley Publishers
116 Pentonville Road
London N1 9JB, UK
and
400 Market Street, Suite 400
Philadelphia, PA 19106, USA

www.jkp.com

Copyright © Mary Korpi 2008

Library of Congress Cataloging in Publication Data
Korpi, Mary.
    Guiding your teenager with special needs through the transition from school to adult life : tools for parents / Mary Korpi.
        p. cm.
    Includes bibliographical references and index.
    ISBN 978-1-84310-874-0 (pbk. : alk. paper) 1. Teenagers with disabilities. 2. Teenagers with disabilities--Services for. 3. Parent and teenager. I. Title.
    HV1569.3.Y68K67 2007
    649'.15--dc22

                                                2007012331

British Library Cataloguing in Publication Data
A CIP catalogue record for this book is available from the British Library

ISBN 978 1 84310 874 0

Printed and bound in the United States by
Thomson-Shore, Inc.

This book is dedicated to people with special needs and their families who courageously stride into the future despite the challenges of adult life.

Acknowledgements

Writing this book gave me the opportunity to put down on paper many of the things that I learned from working with people with special needs and their families. While that has been a satisfying undertaking, the fact of the matter is I have also benefited from extraordinary support and encouragement from the many dedicated professionals with whom I have the privilege to work and from whom I have learned much. In particular a few of these busy and accomplished people took the time to read some *very* rough drafts of an author's first manuscript. I am indebted to them for their interest and generosity.

Lynn Cina MSW, a personal friend as well as a knowledgeable and caring professional, was the first person who took the time to read this manuscript. She encouraged me throughout this experience and spent several summer days reading and editing a very rough first draft. I don't know if I could have continued without her encouragement but I do know this book would not have been as well written or as well grounded as it is had it not included her input.

Two women whom I met through circuitous professional contacts generously volunteered to read a draft of the manuscript. Each of them brought to that reading a wealth of knowledge about this subject. I am awed by their competence and flattered by their interest. However, they did not simply read the book; they took it on as a major project, editing it word by word. Their expertise certainly raised the quality of the contents as well as the cogency with which the information is explained. Many thanks to Dr C. Faith Kappenberg LCSW, a cognitive behavioral psychotherapist and autism consultant specializing in older students with Asperger Syndrome and related learning disabilities. Also to Mrs Barbara Morel, Client Assistance Program Coordinator for Nassau County at the Long Island Advocacy Center, and the parent of a young man with autism spectrum disorder. She often speaks on topics related to advocacy, transition, and parenting a child with autism spectrum disorder.

Finally, I would be negligent if I did not mention the support I received from my family. My youngest son, Kris, never asked me to stop what I was doing to attend to something he wanted. He respected my need to get this done even though neither of us had a clue as to just how much time it would take. My middle son, Kyle, was unfailingly positive in his response to my tentative comments regarding this process. Our eldest, Kevin, and his lovely wife, Miki, who maintained a long distance, if at times skeptical interest in this process. And finally, my husband Emery, who put up with late and no dinners and lots of "not now I just need to finish…" He always responded positively to my requests for his help and I definitely could not have persisted with this were it not for his support.

Contents

Author's Note

I respectfully request that the reader of this book not be put off by the use of the third person – "the child" or "the family." These terms are used in the interest of clarity and consistency. When the focus of the information is more relevant to older people with disabilities, use of the term "the child" may be replaced by "the teenager" or "the young adult" or "the person with a disability." While the author is well aware that an adult child is always a child to his parents, chronologically age-appropriate language supports the theme of this book, which is to encourage the development of essential life skills so that a person with special needs can reach his full potential. Although many parents continue to refer to their adult children as children, in this context it is critically important that our language reflect the maturation of children with special needs.

Despite my strong interest in language that connotes sexual equality I relied on the default position of "he" as the primary pronoun throughout the book. Again the need for clarity and consistency won out over my desire to use less well-known but more inclusive language. The reader will hopefully find the ease of reading the material a satisfactory trade-off.

Disclaimer

Interspersed throughout this book are brief illustrative stories written to highlight specific points. While these stories are based on the author's experiences, they are composites of different people and events. The names and details are changed to protect confidentiality. Any similarities to a person or people are purely coincidental.

Preface

Families often look for information to help them understand a child's special needs. They may use this information to learn new tools that support the child's growth, increase his skills, and improve activities of day-to-day life. Applying new approaches can help the child learn new skills that may allow him more opportunities to participate in the community and live as independently as he is able as he matures. As the child successfully demonstrates new skills, he and the people around him will begin to see him as more competent, which will help increase his self-esteem.

Parents may learn new ideas from a variety of sources including but not limited to books, magazine articles, the Internet, speakers, conferences, and, possibly most satisfying, speaking with other parents. The quantity of information and its complexity can be overwhelming for any parent to absorb. They have to determine what information is relevant to their child's unique situation and then how best to apply it. These decisions can be daunting.

Parents are urged to discuss any new approaches with the professionals who work closely with the child/young adult. The child's medical and/or educational teams are generally in the best position to assist parents when they are learning new tools. These professionals can help determine which tools will facilitate growth and how to implement them with consideration to the child's unique challenges. Professionals working with the family can be a support and a resource. They can help modify techniques so they will meet the unique needs of this child and his family. They can also make adjustments and recommendations in response to any unanticipated events and adapt the plan as progress is made.

Guiding Your Teenager with Special Needs through the Transition from School to Adult Life: Tools for Parents has a dual focus.

Part I, "Family Expectations that Facilitate Growth," looks at some of the steps parents can take to encourage the seeds of independence from a very young age. Specific activities that families may choose to incorporate into their daily lives are discussed with examples of methods for putting these practices into family routines.

Part II, "The School Bus Doesn't Stop Here Any More," describes the complex systems of support available to young adults with special needs as they transition from school and enter post-secondary and adult service programs. It includes essential information regarding financial and legal concerns as well as descriptions of various types of post-secondary and adult programs. Information regarding eligibility requirements, opportunities for training and options for employment are outlined.

Guiding Your Teenager with Special Needs through the Transition from School to Adult Life includes information regarding methods that will enhance the development of essential skills that the child with special needs will rely on throughout his life. It also describes a variety of post-secondary programs and services that a young adult with special needs may require. With this information parents can continue to be effective and knowledgeable advocates with the young adult as he leaves the school system. At the end of each chapter there are lists of sources with specific information regarding the topics covered in that chapter. This additional information will assist families who wish to explore a topic in more detail than is appropriate for this book. These sources may include books, articles, and websites, as well as contact information for relevant agencies and government programs. Key terms are explained in the Notes section on p.133.

PART I

Family Expectations that Facilitate Growth

1

The Parents' Role

Most children learn about adult life through observation and participation in family, social, community, and school-related activities and experiences. They integrate this information and form their own unique understanding of social expectations and their role in the world. Children with special needs are at a significant disadvantage in this process. Often the very nature of the child's disability limits his ability to understand, interpret, and/or assimilate new information. In addition, he may have little community experience, which restricts his opportunity to learn the social expectations of various social and community activities. Generally when parents choose to limit the child's experiences it is meant to protect him, but the fact of the matter is this protection will curb the child's knowledge and understanding of the world in which he lives.

Parents need tools they can use to safely include the child with special needs in a variety of social and community experiences. They need to know how to work with the child's unique learning style and challenges to encourage him to reach his full potential. The information in this book will serve as a starting point for parents to explore methods they may choose to incorporate into family life. Applying these techniques will enhance the child's chance to reach his full potential.

The two most critical times in the education of a child with special needs are during the early intervention period and again when he is preparing to transition out of the school system. Many parents find they need to develop strong advocacy skills in order to obtain medical and/or educational services that best meet the needs of the child. These advocacy skills will be required again, as the child becomes a young adult and prepares to leave the school system. Advocacy is critical in order for a young adult with special needs to have access to a full array of adult opportunities with the essential supports in place.

Parents and school personnel share responsibility to prepare students with disabilities for the demands of adult life. Young adults with special needs must learn how to be safe and at the same time to develop skills that will allow them to reach the highest level of independence that they are capable of achieving. Since students with special needs often require skills, information, and/or social expectations broken down into manageable pieces, the Individuals with Disabilities Education Improvement Act (summarized in Cortiella 2006 and referred to hitherto as IDEIA 2004),[1] a federal law, mandates the inclusion of a specific area for transition planning[2] in every student's Individualized Education Program (IEP)[3] by the year he turns 16 or sooner. The Transition Plan outlines the student's long-term adult outcome, i.e. their plans for the future. It should include steps the student will take to explore his goals, learn new skills, and fine-tune his plans as he acquires knowledge about himself and the world.

Moving from the now familiar and hopefully safe school system into the world of adult services and programs is most often an area of concern for both parents and the young adult. These concerns are well founded. There are legislative mandates that require the school system to provide an appropriate educational program for a child with a disability until the year he turns 21. There is no equivalent mandate for adult services or programs after June of that year. Therefore, once a young adult ages out of the school system it is up to him and his family to navigate adult support systems to find ones that will match his needs. Optimally, participation in the transition planning process has given the young adult multiple opportunities to explore possible goals and to acquire the skills he needs to reach these goals.

When a young adult with a disability is aging out of the school system, parents will need to research the types and quality of programs and services that will best meet his unique needs. This is a critical time when the parent's advocacy skills will once again be required. Therefore, it is essential that parents understand the different types of services, eligibility requirements, and ways of accessing these services. Even parents who have learned to navigate the special education system and be effective advocates for the younger child will find that the processes, philosophies, and funding mechanisms are completely different in the world of adult programs and services, as well as post-secondary education and employment.

Parental advocacy can be even more complex during this transition because the young adult must be actively involved in the process. Decisions need to be made with him rather than for him. The young adult with special needs must be prepared to advocate for himself to the best of his ability. It often comes as a surprise when parents find out that the young adult with a disability must attend all meetings regarding adult programs. Parents may feel like a juggler balancing their own plans, dreams, and expectations with the young adult's wishes and the realities and expectations of adult life. Parents may not be adequately prepared for the shift in their role from primary spokesperson to that of support team member, albeit its most important and optimally most knowledgeable member.

Part II of this book includes an overview of various types of adult programs and services, funding sources, and eligibility requirements. This information will assist parents to advocate effectively *with* the young adult so they can assist him to make informed decisions and prepare for the programs and services that will facilitate opportunities for his continued growth with the necessary level of support.

From the beginning

Parents of children with special needs are often required to speak up to ensure that their child's interests are addressed. There are times when the parent must challenge doctors and other professionals who make recommendations that are inconsistent with the family's goals and/or values. Even when recommendations are based on sound psychological and/or educational principles, they may not fit with the intimate knowledge and unique understanding the parent has of their own child. While adapting to the ups and downs that raising a child with special needs can present, parents must navigate complex systems of support. Parents usually find they need to learn the ins and outs of the special educational system in order to ensure access to educational programs that meet the child's needs.

Attending to the day-to-day care of a child with special needs can present unique challenges for parents. Often these children do not demonstrate age-appropriate behavior. Sometimes families are subjected to rude questions and stares while going about routine activities with the child. For many families, the most difficult aspect of raising a child with special needs is the concern that this child may never achieve the hopes and dreams the parent envisioned for the future. In all likelihood, parents will have to modify their expectations to more closely align with the strengths and interests that the child demonstrates as they transition to adulthood.

To make this Herculean task even more daunting, each child is as unique as are all children. There are children who have challenges that they grow out of. Other children's issues grow as they do. Some behaviors respond to specific interventions while others start families on lifelong quests to find out what works. Children may have physical, emotional, and/or cognitive issues.

Some children's disabilities are an interwoven combination of challenges. The complexity is as distinctive as each individual child. Caring for the child with special needs is not for the faint of heart – but this may not be a voluntary assignment. Children with special needs are members of every type of family and community.

Bearing in mind that each child is unique, there are some overriding expectations that can prepare him to enjoy a fulfilling adult life. First and foremost, the child must learn skills that will allow him to assume as independent a lifestyle as he is capable of. Strategies must be put in place that will build on the child's strengths. These strengths will help him learn new skills and/or modify challenging behaviors. Parents can apply specific techniques that will support the child's development as he matures. Incorporating these techniques into the family's routine will help to ensure consistent application of these effective tools.

Setting high expectations with the appropriate level of support will improve the child's perceived competence in the community as well as in his own eyes. The first step towards accomplishing this goal is for the family and the educational team who work with the child to shift the focus of their interactions from *dis*-ability to *ability*. This shift is critical for the successful implementation of these techniques. Focusing on activities that lead to independence will help to improve the child's self-esteem. This may be accomplished by adding to the skills and knowledge in the child's repertoire. As the child becomes more competent, he will experience a boost in his self-confidence, and increased opportunities to have a positive impact in his personal life, at home, and in the community.

Preparing for life after high school

Optimally, age-appropriate, individualized transition goals are taught from pre-school through high school. The development of a student's IEP should always be based on the acquisition of skills that will enhance the child's independence when he leaves school. IDEIA (2004) requires the inclusion of a Transition Plan in each student's IEP by the time he is 16 years old. This plan should be designed to promote the development of specific core competencies that will support the student as he becomes an adult.

Transition goals may focus on the areas of functional academics, medical and personal care, interpersonal skills, employment, post-secondary education and/or vocational training, community participation, recreational activities, mobility/transportation needs, financial, and legal needs. Goals selected are based on each student's individual strengths and interests. They are organized into a plan of action steps that the student will explore with the support of the educational and community-based team. The transition plan is a dynamic document that changes in response to the student's emerging interests, aptitudes, and competencies.

The Transition Plan needs to focus on skills that will prepare the student for the real world – not simply for success in school. An example of a typical school requirement that does not translate to adult settings follows.

> *In most classrooms students are required to raise their hand and ask to use the bathroom. Raising your hand is not the usual way of indicating the need to use the bathroom in any other setting. For example, employers do not want employees to raise their hand when they wish to use the bathroom at work. Although there may be safety issues regarding students' independent use of the bathroom, requiring a raised hand has nothing to do with teaching the student how to manage the safety issues in a bathroom whether in a school setting or in the community. Schools must examine the skills they are*

> *teaching students through a filter of preparation for real world activities rather than simply "that's how it's always been done."*

The example above highlights how a typical school requirement does not prepare the student for adult life. Transition planning requires schools to adapt their programs and expectations.

Schools are often designed to encourage students to receive information passively and follow teacher-designed routines. In most cases students are not expected to demonstrate initiative or to determine the best approach to a situation. While it is important for students to learn new skills while in school it is perhaps even more important that they develop an understanding of how they learn best. Adults who are able to make accommodations for their own unique challenges are most likely to meet with success outside of the school setting.

Therefore, the student's Transition Plan needs to go beyond traditional classroom activities. It must include opportunities for the acquisition of self-awareness, self-advocacy, and social skills that the young adult will need to live and work in the adult world. As the student prepares to leave the school system the goals need to include methods that support his emerging independence as well as preparation for vocational and post-secondary training opportunities.

Even a well-designed Transition Plan that outlines opportunities for the young adult to acquire the specific competencies he needs to meet his adult goals will be limited without the support of the student's family. The family needs to include the teen in appropriate community experiences and social opportunities that will support the development of social awareness and personal management skills. Participation in a variety of family and community experiences, along with appropriate school-based activities, will optimize the acquisition of the skills that the student needs to achieve the highest level of independence that he is capable of. Again, a good Transition Plan will address this by including the student in the process, making changes as they are needed, and relating the school-based goals to real world expectations.

Further reading and useful resources

Contact a Family (2006) *Contact a Family Fact Sheet: Transition in England and Wales.* Available at www.cafamily.org.uk/transition.html

The George Washington University – National Clearinghouse on Postsecondary Education for Individuals with Disabilities, HEATH Resource Center (2006) *Guidance and Career Counselors' Toolkit – Advising High School Students with Disabilities on Postsecondary Option*s. Available at www.heath.gwu.edu/toolkit/node/223

National Center on Secondary Education and Transition – www.ncset.org

National Dissemination Center for Children with Disabilities (NICHCY) – www.nichcy.org/resources/default.asp

Parent Advocacy Coalition for Educational Rights (PACER) – www.pacer.org

Sicile-Kira, C. (2006) *Adolescents on the Autism Spectrum – A Parent's Guide to the Cognitive, Social, Physical, and Transition Needs of Teenagers with Autism Spectrum Disorders.* New York: Berkley Books, Penguin Group.

Transition map – A roadmap from school to the future for students with disabilities. Philadelphia County School to Work – www.transitionmap.org/schooltowork/philadelphia.htm

2

Developing Responsibility and a Work Ethic

While the development of a sense of self is a complex process, in its simplest form it is based on a child's perception of the impact he has on others. He generally will develop a positive self-esteem when he receives positive feedback in response to his actions. A positive self-esteem supports the child's efforts to try new things and master difficult tasks. This puts the child with special needs and his family at a real disadvantage. A child with a disability will need more support, education, and guidance than might be expected in a typically developing child. Therefore, there may be few naturally occurring opportunities for this child to be relied upon – on the contrary, he may be viewed as one of the many "responsibilities" that family members feel they need to attend to.

So, how can a parent assist a child whose own needs are so great to develop a sense of responsibility? And, really why should they? Doesn't this child have enough going against him without his family making additional demands on him?

In many cases the child who becomes a confident, competent adult is not one whose disability had the least impact on his life, but rather a child whose family has high expectations despite his limitations. Often these are families who *need* the child to step up to the plate and help out to the best of his ability. In some instances, families with fewer resources may require more from every family member. In these families even the child with special needs may be required to meet high expectations. Whether in the area of self-care or pitching in around the house, sometimes these children will have more opportunities to acquire essential life skills and become a responsible, competent family member.

Families with more comfortable lifestyles may not need as much assistance and as a result they may require less of the child with a disability. Ironically, a child whose family has more material resources may be provided with fewer opportunities for him to reach his full potential. In addition, parents who have achieved higher levels of education may be more acutely aware of the limitations that the child's challenges present. This does not have to be the case. Families can choose purposely to incorporate specific discrete techniques designed to improve the child's skills, build his self-confidence, and increase his independence. This type of skill building when approached in a positive and supportive manner will go a long way towards increasing the child's self-esteem.

The task of teaching children with special needs how to become responsible adults is most often accomplished when school personnel and families work together as a team. All aspects of the child's daily life need to assist him as he moves forward towards goals that will become the foundation for him to reach his full potential in adulthood. The following techniques are recommended to help families develop tools and activities that will foster independence, increase competence, and assist in the development of a positive self-esteem. School personnel are encouraged to apply these same techniques in the classroom and community settings in order to facilitate the growth of each child.

That's why they call it work

The ability to persevere when faced with a challenge is essential for people to acquire new skills. With time, proper support, and repeated experiences people can develop the ability to persevere. The fact of the matter is throughout life people are required to perform some essential tasks that they would rather avoid. Performing tasks that are not intrinsically reinforcing is a maturing process. It is a combination of maturity, persistence, and a sense of responsibility that compels a person to keep on trying when faced with the less than enjoyable parts of a job. Acquiring persistence and a sense of responsibility are essential steps for the development of a work ethic.

In the same way that most adults recognize that they need to work in order to get paid, children must learn that sticking with the difficult, unpleasant, and non-reinforcing parts of a task pays off in the long run. This is a very difficult concept for someone who is struggling with his day-to-day needs to understand. Designing a systematic plan *with* the child that incorporates his interests and teaches new skills will support the development of his ability to tolerate increasing levels of frustration. Frustration tolerance is usually essential to achieve mastery of new skills and goals. Reaching desired goals is the backbone for improving self-esteem. People with high self-esteem are more likely to lead healthy, productive lives. Children and adults with special needs are no different in this regard. All children need opportunities to develop a positive self-image in order to reach their full potential.

Notwithstanding the variations in each person's innate personality, families play a major role in the child's development of frustration tolerance, a positive sense of self, and a work ethic. Families can choose to include opportunities to learn new skills into daily family life. Providing the child with supportive and positive learning experiences will improve his chances of achieving his goals and reaching the highest level of independence that he is capable of. Families must establish reasonable expectations and support the child's hard work to reach them. While this task may sound overwhelming, families who are able to provide an initial investment of time and some well thought out planning can expect to achieve positive results within the limitations of the individual child's challenges. Applying the techniques that are explained in this book and refining them to meet each child's unique situation will foster an environment of positive accomplishment and increase opportunities for learning. This is not something that will be achieved overnight but making these techniques part of the fabric or culture of family life will significantly improve the child's skills. This will enhance the quality of life for the child as well as for the people who live and work with him.

Getting started

There are two important decisions a family needs to make in order to set this process in motion. First, they must decide which job the child could learn to do that would be valuable to the family as a whole. This decision needs to be made with the input of the child. Although this is a critical step, it can easily be overlooked. Exploring with the child how he would like to help out or contribute can be the start of shifting attention from "doing for" the child to discovering his abilities and interests. This process is also the first step towards teaching critically important self-advocacy skills that will be needed throughout adult life. Learning to discuss and negotiate household responsibilities will help the child develop the ability to make decisions for himself and to begin to negotiate and explain his preferences.

The second decision families will want to address with the child is the selection of rewards or reinforcers. Initially rewards should immediately follow the completion of the job or the part of the job that the child is learning to do. For example, if the child enjoys playing a particular video game – which has been time limited until now – more time on this game can be contingent upon his taking out the trash or whatever part of the chore he has agreed to learn.

Some children will not cooperatively take on new chores. Parents may need to remind the child of the benefits of learning new tasks. If the child has prior associations with working or even learning as something at which he is not successful, parents will want to be sure that the child understands the new and different approach that they are now using. First, the child needs to believe that he is able to learn this new task; second, he must feel certain that he will receive positive support throughout the experience; and third, that he can count on receiving the pre-selected reward for cooperating with this new experience. Most often the best way to get someone to understand something is to demonstrate it. Therefore, parents may want to gradually introduce an activity based on fun rather than on work. Parents need to make sure that the child's portion of the job is "bite-sized" and that positive reinforcement is liberally applied while the child is learning a new task. Verbal praise for the child's efforts, not just for his successes, will be essential. Parents can then slowly increase the number of steps the child is responsible for while maintaining close contact and support.

For some children simply explaining how their help will improve the family is enough to get started. In any case, parents need to be careful not to use the child's new skills as an opportunity to go off and accomplish another task. He must receive the positive reinforcement that was agreed to. Spending time together doing family fun activities, or spending time alone with a parent, are two powerful reinforcers for many children. Other children will rather earn extra time doing a preferred activity such as watching TV or playing a video game. Parents should carefully guard the child's right to receive and enjoy the reward he has earned. After all, how many adults would accept a cut in their paychecks when they make a mistake at work or if a co-worker needed the money more than them? This is what a child experiences when the parent take away his reinforcer because of some further misdeed or because of the demands of another child.

Parents will want to be careful not to assume that the child knows how to perform the selected job. Parents need to remember that the child with special needs will most likely learn best when tasks are broken down into specific discrete steps that are presented in the modality that supports the child's unique learning style. For example, some children will respond to verbal directions while others may need written or picture schedules. Physical demonstration or modelling of a task is often the most effective method of teaching a new skill. Repetition is almost always essential for true skill acquisition. Some children may be able to do a task one day and appear to have forgotten it the next time. Parents will need to develop a variety of methods to remind the child of what he needs to do. Ongoing parental support throughout the learning process will generally be most effective. A positive supportive learning environment will help the child make the association that learning new things and working are positive experiences and therefore worth overcoming the initial challenges.

Now for the caveats...

1. The reinforcer must be something he does not currently have independent access to. (If he is currently permitted unlimited time playing video games then the concept of earning it will understandably not be perceived as a positive thing. Reinforcement must be more time or new access or a new item.)

2. The child must want the reinforcer.

3. Initially, the reinforcer should be immediate and readily available – eventually the child can earn

points towards a larger long-term reinforcer such as purchasing a desired item, or more game/TV/computer time.

4.   The parent must follow through with their side of the agreement.

5.   A pleasant, positive tone throughout this interaction is essential so the child will associate learning a new activity with a positive experience.

6.   Clear explanations/demonstrations/modeling/ written and/or picture schedules will go a long way to guide him through the task at a level that approaches your expectations. Some children may require a series of photographs of them going through each of the tasks or a written checklist in the required order. Most often the parent will need to demonstrate each step and/or give verbal reminders along the way.

Gradually the child needs to take the lead in these interactions; this allows him to develop a sense of accomplishment that becomes its own reward. This can take a *very* long time to emerge. In the short run, this is going to cost the parent more time and attention than doing the task alone. *But*, and here's the final caveat...

7.   The child's self-esteem will flourish due to his increased sense of mastery and accomplishment and from the positive attention he receives.

Working together, the parent and child can decide how best to approach each new responsibility. Deciding which jobs to work on will help to shift the family's focus from what the child can't do to figuring out what he can learn. Strategies will need to be developed that build on the child's current strengths and skills in order to facilitate reaching his next goal. The family will begin to focus on what is being accomplished, how to support the process, and how to build on the success.

A good example of this follows:

> *Mandee's parents wanted to find ways to build their ten-year-old daughter's sense of responsibility. Up to this point Mandee could pretty much get anything she pointed to. Her vocabulary was increasing, slowly – physically she was fairly adept, though small for her age. Mandee's parents sat down with her for a serious talk about the fact that she was growing up and needed to help out. They pointed out how other family members contribute and how this helps their family have more time for fun things.*
>
> *At the suggestion of Mandee's occupational therapist, Mandee and her parents decided that setting the table every night would be a task that she could learn to do and talked with Mandee about possible reinforcement for learning to do this new job. She decided that what she most wanted was time alone with her mom. Since they both could use a little exercise, an after dinner walk (just for mom and Mandee) would be Mandee's reinforcement for setting the table.*
>
> *Learning to set the table presented Mandee and her family with many strategic challenges. Mandee had to learn how to count the number of people eating and match that to the number of plates needed. Initially, Mandee's mom handed her each plate, once Mandee told her the number that was needed. Mandee's mom helped her check if the number she counted was correct, but allowed her to make mistakes from time to time. The natural consequence of not having enough place settings for everyone provided Mandee with the opportunity to internalize how important her job was to her family. The inconvenience of having to get up and get the place setting that was missing reinforced Mandee's desire to count correctly in the future.*

> *After a few weeks, Mandee no longer needed her mom to count out the plates with her, but she couldn't reach where they were stored. Mandee asked if the plates could be kept in the bottom cabinet so she could get them out herself. Mandee demonstrated initiative, problem-solving, and the desire for independence with this simple request.*
>
> *Mandee was becoming frustrated with the amount of help she still needed to figure out where to place the utensils. Mandee's brother remembered making placemats in nursery school that outlined the proper placement of utensils. Mandee and her brother sat down together and designed a special placemat for each member of their family. Mandee's mom reported that this was the first time Mandee's brother volunteered to spend time with Mandee.*

In the above example, Mandee's family applied many of the recommended techniques that led to a successful experience. They discussed the plan with Mandee's educational team and decided that setting the table was a skill Mandee could learn that was essential to family life and that had a natural consequence. Most important, it was an activity that Mandee had shown an interest in learning. By including Mandee's educational team, Mandee was able to receive additional practice at school when she worked with the occupational therapist on this goal. Using the skill in a different location helped Mandee to acquire the skill more quickly.

Mandee's family discussed the activity and the reinforcement with Mandee prior to starting even though Mandee may not have been capable of completing understanding the process. Her input was sought at each step along the way. Mandee's mom introduced one aspect of the job i.e. placing one dish at each chair while mom continued to perform the rest of the job herself. They modified the environment to meet Mandee's needs (changed where the dishes were stored so she could reach them).

And, with her brother, Mandee made placemats that outlined the position of each object. These placemats are a template or model for Mandee. Now Mandee has a way to check that she has remembered each part of the job without relying on mom to check and correct her work. She also gained a new opportunity to problem-solve whenever an item didn't match the placemat.

The following list illustrates the skills and benefits Mandee and her family reported as a result of using these techniques:

- skills learned
    - table setting
    - one-to-one matching
    - reinforcement of counting
    - sequencing
    - patterning skills
- emotional benefits
    - improved family dynamics
    - Mandee and mom spend positive time together and get a little exercise
    - Mandee begins to assume a more responsible role within her family
    - Mandee's family views her as more competent
    - Mandee begins the process of maturing into a responsible working person.

Even though this is an impressive list of skills, Mandee's most significant gain is in her sense of self. Mandee and her family were slowly able to shift from viewing her as someone who needed to be cared for to someone who could be relied on. Mandee's improved sense of self has manifested itself in many other areas including her willingness to try new tasks in the classroom. Mandee's experience also highlights the shift in family dynamics that can take place as the result of a well-designed "chore."

There are many other family activities even young children can learn to do with the appropriate level of support and reinforcement. Emptying the dishwasher is a wonderful patterning skill (placing items where they belong). It is a job that has a clear beginning and end point. It can also be performed when the child chooses, but before the next meal. This decreases the need for parents to remind the child to get the job done. If the dishwasher is not emptied by the next meal the child will need to be called away from whatever he is doing at that moment and help out. However, the child can be assisted to set up a schedule when it will be best for him and for the family so the clean dishes are ready before each meal. Again, parents may need to be very involved with the child as they learn to do this task as well as to set up a schedule that is mutually agreeable.

Matching socks, folding and putting clothing away, taking out trash, and replacing trash bags are more examples of household tasks that can be learned by young children. As the child gains expertise in some of these basic areas, additional chores such as doing laundry, vacuuming, dusting, and making basic meals can be taught and added to the child's weekly list of responsibilities.

Reinforcers

Immediate reinforcement will be essential while the child is learning a new task. It is important to begin with low cost items that the child values so they can receive the reinforcer as agreed upon without bankrupting the family. Parents may wish to include preferred activities that the child can choose as alternative reinforcers. Immediate reinforcement needs to lead gradually to a system of delayed reinforcement. It is essential that the child develop the ability to delay reinforcement in order to be able to function in a paying job. Visual reminders such as star charts or checklists can be very useful for the child to gain an understanding of the steps that are needed to receive the larger reinforcement.

Families may wish to incorporate "special time" or activities as part of a reinforcement plan. The example of Mandee above shows one way that special time with a parent can be a reward for positive behavior. Some families develop a system whereby the child can have a certain period of time with the parent or family member of their choice for a pre-determined accomplishment or behavior. However, the child can choose which activity they want to do when they are with that adult if they have demonstrated the new skill or behavior with a positive attitude and/or without special reminders. But if the chore was accomplished with a poor attitude or with extra reminders, support, and/or assistance, the child still gets the time with the adult but the adult chooses the activity.

> *William gets 30 minutes before bed with his dad every night he empties the dishwasher. Now that William consistently demonstrates mastery of the skills involved in emptying the dishwasher he needs to initiate and complete this task to an agreed upon standard with no more than the agreed upon reminders. If he does this he gets to choose which activity he wants to do with dad. Generally, William chooses to watch TV, play a video game, or race his toy cars. However, if William required several reminders to empty the dishwasher before dinner, does the job incorrectly or with a poor attitude, dad gets to choose. He may pick out a book for the two of them to read together, take a walk, or play catch.*

In the example above, William has learned all of the steps he needs to perform a chore successfully, and he gets positive reinforcement for doing it correctly. However, he is given an additional opportunity to make choices about the quality of the reinforcement when he does the chore independently. Many families find adding this nuance to the plan goes a long way to ensuring that the child takes on the chore as his own responsibility rather than continually needing to be reminded to get the chore done.

At some point it is important to introduce money as reinforcement for the completion of some of the chores. This helps the child make the connection between work and money and to learn the value of money. Children find it easier to make this association if they have been involved in making purchases with the parent, even if using the parent's money or money they received as a gift. Earning money towards making a larger purchase teaches the benefit of delayed gratification. This is a critical competency for successful employment but one that many children take years to truly incorporate. A clear, understandable chart that outlines specific steps towards reaching the long-term goal is a recommended method to teach this connection. The child can place a star or check on the chart at the successful completion of each step, with a certain number signifying that the goal is reached and they have earned the reward they were working for.

In some families children receive a weekly allowance for doing their own laundry and/or cleaning their own room. Once these tasks are mastered, some families choose to provide opportunities for the child to earn additional money by learning and completing additional chores. This is a slow process that will occur over many years. As the child grows into a teenager it is important to build on the competencies they have acquired. Activities such as vacuuming other rooms in the house, gardening, cleaning the bathroom or kitchen, etc. may be added to the teen's chores. This will increase his skills, as well as his opportunities to make money. Learning to pair working with earning is a maturing process that supports the development of a work ethic. The ability to persevere in a job despite how you feel at the moment is essential for successful employment later in life.

Parents may find that the child or teen who is accustomed to getting everything he asks for will likely find it extremely difficult to internalize the need to postpone receiving a desired item. This will hinder his ability to persevere when faced with a challenging task even when he wants the reward. The child who is accustomed to getting what he wants given to him may expect that he will receive the desired item without having to earn it. It can be extremely difficult for a child who has been indulged in this way to learn to work for money. While it may be easy for parents to purchase items at the request of the child, this indulgence can become a major roadblock to the development of a work ethic. The child who expects to have his every request met is not learning the value of working for his own money.

Understanding the connection between working and money is generally essential for the development of a work ethic. As the child acquires the concept of money, parents will want to provide them with opportunities for delaying gratification. Saving money towards a larger item will improve the child's ability to delay a reward. Some children and teens enjoy setting up a bank account in their own name and depositing money regularly. Others prefer to store the money at home in a safe place so they can retrieve it and count it themselves. In either case the child needs to be encouraged to save the money to purchase a larger item, go on a preferred outing, or even donate part of it to others who are in greater need. Saving money for a large purchase teaches budgeting skills and fosters the development of working towards a long-term goal.

The importance of teaching each new task in a positive, supportive manner cannot be over-emphasized. Parents should expect to be integrally involved in the completion of each of the chores until the child can comfortably accomplish the task on their own. Parents need to assess which part of the job the child is able to do and gradually reduce their assistance with this step while remembering to praise the child's effort and achievement.

Positive feedback that is appropriate to the child's needs generally is the most powerful tool that the parent can use. Telling the child verbally, physically affirming their effort with a smile or a pat on the back, or even allowing them to overhear you praise their work when speaking with others, are all generally excellent methods of reinforcing the child's efforts to learn a new skill.

The next critical point in this process is when the child begins to demonstrate mastery of the task. Now the parent needs to step slowly out of the supportive role. Careful attention will be required to decrease the amount of parental help systematically while continuing to provide reinforcement for a job successfully completed.

There are times when a child begins to rely so heavily on the positive attention that it actually slows down the child's progress towards independence. Some children may continue to seek out a parent's help beyond the real need for them to learn the task. Most often this is an attempt to continue to receive the positive attention the parent is giving the child while they are learning something new. Parents need to provide opportunities to spend quality time with the child upon completion of a chore. When positive interactions continue while attention is gradually reduced during the activity, the child will begin to associate task completion with positive experiences. This will build a desire for independence.

On the other hand, parents should remember that the child might genuinely need more support to acquire a new skill. Parents should try to step back and look closely at how much help they are actually providing when they work with the child. Sometimes the child can become dependent on this help and not truly acquire the skill. Even non-verbal cues can be reinforcing. Parents may need to slowly physically move away from the activity. Some children will accept this change more easily if the parent makes an excuse for leaving the room such as "I need to get my glasses, I'll be right back." Parents can then gradually increase the time the child is working on his own. The parent should make every effort to return to the child and praise his work before he calls out for help or stops working. Again, slowly increasing the time away but always providing positive reinforcement is critical to the success of this process.

There are also children who are not reinforced by positive attention. This may be due to the nature of the child's disability or because his developmental stage is such that he is not reinforced by interactions with other people or specifically by attention from his parents. When this is the case parents will want to rely even more heavily on systematic charts that clearly delineate the steps needed to reach short-term and long-term goals. Creating a visual picture of each step in the job and the order in which to complete them will support the child as he works. Clear and systematic routine steps are essential for the child to achieve independence at a task. There may be two different charts. One chart outlines each step of the job, while the other lists the goals and the reinforcers for achieving those goals.

There are many different methods that can be used to provide the child with the support they need to master a new job. Charts listing each step, drawings or pictures that can be cut out of a magazine, or actual photographs of the child performing each step can work as visual reminders of what must be done to complete a chore. Children who are auditory learners may respond to wearing a headset with taped directions of each step. They can start or stop the tape as they go through the chore. For example, a job coach[6] when working with a student who was a non-reader used this method very successfully. The student was unable to remember to perform every part of a multi-step job. She taped herself talking him through each part of the job. She even included extra tips like, "Don't forget to sweep behind the door" and "Before you leave the room, stop and look back to make sure you really have completed every task for this room."

Including the child in the creation of these tools and charts is essential for them to understand what is expected of them and to feel ownership of the system that is in place.

Emotional concerns

It is essential for parents to seek support and information about the child's behavior in order to maintain a positive focus and to develop new strategies in response to any unanticipated occurrences that may come up during this process. Parent groups can be an invaluable source of support as well as regular meetings with a knowledgeable, caring professional who understands the child's specific challenges as well as the family dynamics.

Some parents may feel uncomfortable or even guilty for requiring the child with a disability to meet high expectations. This is unfortunate for both the child and his family. Providing opportunities to acquire new skills and competencies with the supports the child needs builds self-esteem. The role of the child in the family can change from that of the one who needs to be cared for to that of an active, contributing member of the family. Through these experiences the child gains maturity and a sense of responsibility that will serve him well throughout adult life. Completing an agreed upon chore, even when a person doesn't feel like it, teaches perseverance. It cannot be over-emphasized how valuable the development of the ability to persevere is for the development of a work ethic and for enhancing a child's sense of self.

Further reading

Baker, B. and Brithman, A. (1997) *Steps to Independence: Teaching Everyday Skills to Children with Special Needs*. Baltimore, MD: Paul H. Brookes Publishing.

Delmolino, L. and Harris, S. (2004) *Incentives for Change: Motivating People with Autism Spectrum Disorders to Learn and Gain Independence*. Bethesda, MD: Woodbine House.

Howlin, P. and Baron-Cohen, S. (1998) *Teaching Children with Autism to Mind-Read: A Practical Guide for Teachers and Parents.* London: John Wiley and Sons.

Richfield, S. and Bochert, C. (2003) *The Parent Coach: A New Approach to Parenting in Today's Society.* Longmont, CO: Sopris West.

3

Learning Skills
That Lead to Independence

In order for a person with special needs to become an active part of the adult community they must be able to understand and interpret appropriate community behaviors. With careful, well thought out planning most people with special needs can gain many of the essential competencies that will allow them the opportunity to safely access their community as adults. The process of learning social skills and community behavior is generally a long and gradual one. Safety considerations make this an area of particular concern for all involved. The families of people with special needs are uniquely qualified to provide social opportunities and support that will facilitate learning skills that are essential to being an active member of the community.

Although the idea of teaching social competence and the tools that will facilitate learning these skills may initially be new and unfamiliar to most families, it can become a routine part of how the family approaches each new experience. Families need to determine the types of community settings that are interesting to the child or young adult with special needs and then break down the steps that go into participating in these settings. Family members may need to consult with the professionals who work closely with the child or young adult to identify which skills should be focused on first. As the person with special needs gains experience in this process their input will be essential for continuing success. However, in order to assure ongoing opportunities for learning new skills, the family must incorporate these new approaches into the fabric of their daily routine. With experience, some families become so adept at these skills that they are able to assess each new situation quickly and determine the best approach for the child.

For example, an activity such as ordering take out food can provide many learning opportunities that when done with the appropriate level of support, will teach new skills and foster a sense of competence regarding community use. The following list illustrates some of the activities that go into this routine chore that support the acquisition of new skills:

- deciding which type of take out food from which restaurant
- finding the menu
- checking with each family member as to their preferences i.e. taking orders
- calling the restaurant
- placing the order
- determining what time to leave to pick it up
- estimating the amount the purchase will be
- deciding how much money to bring
- traveling to the restaurant to pick up the food
- going into the restaurant and greeting the workers appropriately
- stating the name used when ordering
- paying for the order

- carrying the order to the car

- bringing the order into the house

- alerting other family members that the food has arrived

- gathering the utensils that will be needed.

This activity is rich with opportunities for mastery of many essential skills, including but not limited to:

- telephone skills

- organizational skills

- greeting skills

- money skills

- safe and appropriate behavior in the community.

Parents need to remember to include the person with special needs when selecting an activity and to decide which part of the task they wish to learn first. Parents will also want to decide how much support will be needed for the person to acquire the new skill and feel successful. This experience can be the first of many that will require negotiation and compromise for all concerned.

Parents are urged to be cautious about relying on group activities that the person with special needs participates in as the primary method for him to acquire the skills he will need to function in the community. Even people who are involved in community-based school and/or recreational programs will not necessarily gain the competencies needed to access the community on their own. Being part of a group, people often follow along and may not internalize the skill sets, decision-making, and/or problem-solving tools that are required to achieve true independence in the community. The family is in a unique position to provide meaningful experiences that will build a social repertoire with the child based on his unique needs and interests.

The keys to the kingdom: planning, preparation, and practice

Deciding what type of community activity to start with and how to proceed from that point is a decision that should be made by the parent together *with* the child, not *for* him. It is essential that all parties feel the outings are successful so that a positive association develops regarding learning these skills. Parents can then build upon the positive activities and introduce new experiences. The following include some of the places parents might first think of when beginning this process: the supermarket, convenience store, bank, or post office. However, there are other community settings that are likely to be more reinforcing for a child. Going to video stores, fast food restaurants, and toy stores are more likely to be of interest to a child or young adult. These highly reinforcing environments may add incentive for the child to overcome initial resistance or discomfort when learning a new skill such as asking a store employee where an item is located.

Prior to the outing parents will explain that this is not a shopping experience but rather a learning and looking trip. Therefore, neither the child nor the parent will be making any purchases at this time. However, a purchase can be made at another time preferably using money the child has earned. This will facilitate the development of the ability to delay gratification and add incentive for the child to want to earn money by performing chores at home. A little frustration will enhance the development of the concept of delayed gratification. Initially, parents may need to return to the car to avoid an outburst if the child starts to become too frustrated or upset. They can then decide together whether to return to the store at this time or later. Again, the keys to success are clear expectations, preparation, practice, and limiting the length of time for the outing. Applying these tools will help make this a positive learning experience.

Deciding on a specific goal for the outing provides a clear sense of purpose and structure that will help determine the success of the new experience. Building on success will further the growth of self-esteem. For example, going to a video store to rent a specific video is an example of a highly reinforcing short outing that can be motivating enough to encourage direct interaction with store employees. Parents will identify with the child which skill they want the child to work on, explain and/or practice this skill, and determine the level of support that may be needed.

For example, if the child is working on phone skills, he can call the video store and find out if a certain movie or game is available. The following steps should be helpful to determine the degree of support the child will need to be successful in this activity:

1. Write out a script of what to say and how the other person is likely to respond.

2. Practice the script with the parent.

3. Practice the phone call with a relative.

4. Call the store with the parent on the extension and standing in the same room.

5. Call the store with the parent on the extension but in another room (parents may wish to manipulate this process by starting off in the same room and then telling the child they need to go into another part of the house to retrieve something).

6. Call the store without the parent on the extension.

When doing this activity with the child parents may find that all of these steps are not necessary *or* that there are other steps that need to be included. The amount of support a child needs to acquire a new skill depends on his level of understanding and experience. Therefore, parents must be prepared to support the child in a manner that facilitates the development of the skill *and* the confidence to perform the skill on his own. Parents should take note of the child's response to each step and apply this knowledge when introducing the next new learning experience. Each new skill will require planning and preparation, but in most cases as the child matures and acquires a greater repertoire of experience the amount and type of planning will decrease.

In order to begin this process, the parent and child select which community activity to start with. Next, it is essential to talk about the kinds of things one might expect to find in this setting and to outline socially appropriate behavior. Many families find techniques such as "story boarding"[4] or Social Stories™[5] can be useful in these situations. Hoekman (2006) explains that story boarding involves developing an outline of each step of an activity before it is tried. This can be done with pictures, in writing, orally, and/or through acting out roles, depending on the person's learning style and abilities. Social Stories™, written according to the guidelines and criteria developed by Carol Gray, involve writing out a description of an activity including the child's expected role. The parent will read the story to or with the child on many occasions prior to beginning the new experience.

The benefit of both these techniques is that they allow people to practice the activities and expectations of an experience before doing it. This is an extension of a common mental exercise that many people in the general population rely on, referred to as "mental rehearsal." Mentally rehearsing events prior to participating in them will help to increase a person's comfort level. People with special needs, and for that matter, anyone with limited life experiences may benefit from specifically drawn outlines that can be "rehearsed" or practiced prior to participating in an experience. Parents will want to establish a positive, upbeat, and supportive tone throughout this experience.

Once the planned activity is outlined and/or discussed a quick review of the expectations immediately prior to starting may be helpful. Again, parents will want to clearly identify the child's role in the activity. The more clearly the child's role is delineated, the more likely he will understand it, which will greatly improve the chance of it being a successful experience. It is also important to go over the goal of the outing and to decide on the length of time that it will take. Initially, very short and specific timeframes can be crucial for success. It is essential that parents treat this as a teaching experience, not one in which personal chores are likely to be accomplished.

Steps for success will include:

1. Decide with the child which activity is mutually interesting.

2. Lay out each of the steps using the technique that best meets the child's learning style and comprehension level; the smaller the step the more readily it can be assimilated.

3. Select with the child which part of the activity they would like to focus on.

4. Select with the child the reward or reinforcer they will receive for their success.

5. Clearly define what constitutes success.

6. Set up a contingency or back-up plan for unexpected outcomes.

7. Remain positive and supportive throughout!

As these experiences are incorporated into the child's repertoire, parents will want to look for opportunities to decrease the amount of support they provide in some of the familiar community businesses.

When the child is ready to make a purchase, the following steps can be used to increase his independence in this highly reinforcing activity:

- Prepare a list of purchases for each store.

- Estimate the cost of items and decide how much money will be needed.

- Decide which purchases the child is responsible for and have him place the amount of money needed in his own wallet. (Some young people will decide what to give the cashier by using a technique called the next highest dollar, that is, round up the amount to the next full dollar. Others may need exact change, depending on the young person's understanding of money.)

- Have the child carry the item/s he has purchased.

Initial support throughout the process may be called for, but the goal is to reduce the level of support gradually, eventually allowing the child or teen to lead the interaction.

There are many skills that are acquired through repeated experiences and participation in community living. The following list identifies some of the skills that can be the focus of this type of experience:

- planning

- preparing a list

- budgeting

- making choices

- personal responsibility for safely storing money

- organizing and categorizing to find desired items

- scanning the aisle and choosing the appropriate items

- locating an available cashier

- appropriate waiting behavior

- communication with the cashier, other store employees, and customers

- using a wallet

- money skills

- retrieval and replacement of money at a socially acceptable pace.

When the child consistently demonstrates competence with you present it is time for parents to start "fading,"[7] that is, slowly decreasing the amount of support they provide for the part of the activity the young person has learned. Allowing an increase in the physical distance between the parent and the child is the first step in the fading process. The following example demonstrates this method:

> *Terrance is a 15-year-old with special needs who enjoys video games. He and his dad have been making weekly trips to the local game store where Terrance has gradually learned how to make selections, who to speak with when he can't find his selection, how to wait on line, to get his money ready, to choose the correct amount of money and when to give it to the cashier (using next highest dollar), to wait for change, pick up his package, and walk out of the store. "Today when we go to the video store I will wait outside for you," explains Terrance's dad.*
>
>   *Prior to going into the store, Terrance and his dad review the steps Terrance will use to make his purchase. Terrance's dad assures him that he will be waiting outside. He instructs*

Terrance to come out and get him at any time if he feels unsure about what to do. Although Terrance is apprehensive about this next step, he rises to the occasion and is successful at making his purchase. Terrance was able to accomplish this step towards independence through repeated practice in this personally desirable community environment.

Terrance and his dad decide to go to a fast food restaurant for lunch following his success. As Terrance grows more comfortable with this task, his father's verbal praise and sharing Terrance's success with the important people in his life becomes the secondary reinforcement. Terrance's purchase is his primary reinforcer.

Terrance and his father repeat this experience for several more weeks with no problems. Terrance's father then tells him that while Terrance is in the video store he will go into the stationery store next door. He shows Terrance where the stationery store is in relation to the game store. As he walks him to the game store they synchronize their watches and review their meeting place. After a few weeks of success, Terrance's dad varies the routine by setting up alternative meeting places and extending the time Terrance is left on his own. The eventual goal is to drop Terrance off and pick him up at a pre-determined time.

Many families find it helpful to use these techniques prior to all family activities and outings as they allow a person with special needs to practice social norms of the varied social experiences they may encounter. People need opportunities to prepare and plan for experiences in order to learn how they will be expected to behave. It often is valuable to review the skills that are required for a specific event just before it occurs even when a measure of competence was demonstrated the last time. Most people will require multiple experiences to incorporate a new behavior truly into their repertoire. Practicing how to say hello and goodbye, in what situations and with whom to shake hands and/or hug, and even specific ideas for topics of conversation or questions will be helpful. Tools such as Social Stories™, story boarding, focused discussions, and/or role-playing can be useful to prepare for social expectations prior to the actual event.

Safety

Safety awareness is critical for anyone to responsibly participate independently in the community. Parents should continue to reinforce awareness of strangers and who to trust. Problem-solving practice will be needed to build a repertoire of possible responses to unexpected situations. For example, playing "What if…?" type games can serve as a gentle reminder of how to handle unexpected events.

A cell phone is invaluable for this type of independence training in the community. The young adult will need to know how to use the cell phone so he can speed dial to reach you at any point in the process. As with all new skills, practice using the cell phone at home, in the car, in stores, etc. This will help incorporate calling on the cell phone into his repertoire. The goal is for the young person to develop an automatic response to dial the cell phone whenever there is an unexpected occurrence and/or he is not sure what to do.

Moving on to larger community settings

As a person gains competence, families will want to encourage the use of their new community-based independence skills in larger community businesses such as supermarkets and/or malls. Some families start by asking the child to get an item from the next aisle when they are shopping. As he gains confidence and skills, he may take responsibility for a part of the shopping list, push his own cart, and pay with his own money (even if the parent has given it to him earlier). Supermarkets are wonderful environments to practice:

- reading/matching skills – searching for specific items on shelves

- categorizing skills – determining where to find specific items by reading the aisle signs

- focusing skills in environments that are often over-stimulating

- appropriate behavior for waiting in line

- making purchases.

A higher level of independence will be needed to navigate malls. Parents will want to start off at a familiar store that the teen wishes to frequent. Gradually over several visits parents can increase the physical distance between themselves and the teen. The parent and teen can set up meeting times and places of increasing length and distance. For example, while the teen looks at the DVDs, the parent can head off to men's clothing and agree to meet up at a designated place and time. It is important that the child knows where the parent will be and that they agree to stay within a pre-determined area while they are separated from the parent. Use of the cell phone will be invaluable in this setting. (Be sure to check to confirm that cell phone reception is available.)

Malls are typically social experiences for all teens. The teen with special needs might feel more comfortable if he invites a friend to join him at the mall. Sharing the experience with a like-minded friend can be reassuring for all concerned. Parents may need to take an active role in setting up social experiences for the teen with special needs. This is another area where parents will want to apply the techniques described above to reduce their role gradually as the teen acquires skills and becomes confident in his ability to use them.

Leaving the teen in a public place with a pre-arranged meeting time and location will reinforce the importance of effective time telling skills. The teen will have to practice reading the time, as well as how to estimate the length of time needed to accomplish something, and then be aware enough to rendezvous as planned. These are essential skills for a working adult as well. Many jobs require workers to take lunch and breaks at specific times. The worker must be able to determine when he needs to return to the job and to estimate the length of time he has to accomplish what he wants to during his break. If he is unable to keep track of time, the use of a watch that can be set to beep after a pre-determined length of time can address this challenge.

With increasing community experiences, parents will want to ensure that the young person with special needs can safely navigate an active parking lot, street crossings, and possibly learn to use public transportation or a para-transit system. Although IDEA[1] mandates that schools provide opportunities for students to develop travel skills, parents may wish to work with the teen's school or agency staff and reinforce the development of the skills they will need to access the community. Due to liability issues, schools and other organizations will rarely allow an individual independent use of the community while they are under their auspices. Parents need to find ways to provide as many experiences of pedestrian crossings and public transportation as they wish the person with special needs to have.

Although some people with special needs will learn to drive, many will rely on public transportation. Independent use of the community's public transportation system is the means to independence for many people with a significant disability. Most communities have a transit-transit system. This is a system that provides door-to-door transportation at rates higher than public transportation but less than a private taxi service. Even people who will rely on a transit-transit service need to learn how to keep themselves safe in the community.

The tools outlined in this chapter allow families to identify essential, routine, and enjoyable activities they can choose to focus on. Combining these activities with systematic teaching experiences will increase a young person's independence in the community. Incorporating learning experiences into the family's culture will go a long way to ensure consistent opportunities to build skills.

Further reading

Cornish, U. and Ross, F. (2003) *Social Skills Training for Adolescents with General Moderate Learning Difficulties.* London: Jessica Kingsley Publishers.

Smith Myles, B., Trautman, M.L. and Schelvan, R.L. (2004) *The Hidden Curriculum: Practical Solutions for Understanding Unstated Rules in Social Situations.* Shawnee Missions, KS: Autism Asperger Publishing.

Wehman, P. (2006) *Life Beyond the Classroom: Transition Strategies for Young People with Disabilities, 4th edition.* Baltimore, MD: Paul H. Brookes Publishing Company.

Williams, M. and Shellenberger, S. (1996) *How Does Your Engine Run? A Leader's Guide to the Alert Program for Self-regulation.* Albuquerque, NM: Therapy Works.

4

New Areas to Explore

Depending on the nature of the child's disability, early adolescence may present the family with new challenges. While some children at this age wish to remain in the protective cocoon of family and school life, many others begin to challenge every demand placed upon them. In either case, this is the time when parents must introduce the idea that the young teen is growing up and needs to learn social and age-appropriate norms for personal grooming and behavior in public.

Personal hygiene

Physical changes are likely to accelerate in adolescence and may present the teenager with special needs and their families with some unique challenges. Teaching self-care skills can require a parent to exercise huge amounts of diplomacy and tact. Parents must clearly communicate adult expectations for grooming while respecting the teenager's increased need to assert their independence.

In all likelihood parents will need to take an active role to teach the teenager how to perform personal routines of an intimate nature. A teenager may be unaware of the need for more frequent showers, use of deodorant, hair and skin care. Many parents find grooming checklists paired with rewards for successful completion to be a useful tool. Some families set up a routine whereby the teenager is required to complete their grooming routine early in the evening in order to earn the right to watch a particular show or have additional game time. This is a good example of how to incorporate adult expectations with family routines.

Just as in teaching the skills needed to complete household chores, parents need to be careful about assuming children understand the essential steps involved in personal grooming. Questions as to how much of a product is needed to accomplish a task, how often to wash and to shave, and the special needs of a young woman during her cycle must be addressed with clear, specific guidelines and praise for follow through. Complex, and for some families embarrassing, topics must be addressed in order for the young teen to gain the competencies they will need to fit into adult society.

Privacy

It is essential that the teenager begin to understand that they are becoming an adult and therefore they need to begin to meet adult expectations of behavior. The family must set clear guidelines for privacy such as closing doors when performing personal routines in order for the teenager with special needs to incorporate this behavior into his repertoire. At the same time it may be necessary for the parent to be physically present while the teen is learning sophisticated personal hygiene skills. Parents may wish to introduce the concepts of self-care and privacy before the child is an adolescent so that the teen will require minimal assistance when the need for personal care increases.

When the teen is seeking greater independence from the parent he may be highly motivated to demonstrate competence in these activities. On the other hand, the teen that is not yet striving for independence may need his parents to slow down the pace of their expectations so they will match his capabilities. However, it is important that parents not lose sight of the fact that the teen is becoming an adult and as such should be expected to move towards adult-type personal care routines and to surround himself with chronologically age-appropriate clothing, hair styles, and accessories.

Further reading

Lieberman, L. (2005) *A "Stranger" Among Us: Hiring In-Home Support for a Child with Autism Spectrum Disorders or Other Neurological Differences.* Shawnee Mission, KS: Autism Asperger Publishing Company.

Notbohm, E. and Zysk, V. (2004) *1001 Great Ideas for Teaching and Raising Children with Autism Spectrum Disorders.* Arlington, TX: Future Horizons.

Sicile-Kira, C. (2006) *Adolescents on the Autism Spectrum – A Parent's Guide to the Cognitive, Social, Physical, and Transition Needs of Teenagers with Autism Spectrum Disorders.* New York: Berkley Books, Penguin Group.

Wrobel, M. (2003) *Taking Care of Myself: A Hygiene, Puberty and Personal Curriculum for Young People with Autism.* Arlington, TX: Future Horizons.

5

Transition Planning

As the teenager moves into the uncharted territory of late adolescence there is renewed urgency for parents to advocate in order to ensure that the young adult's changing needs are addressed. The IDEIA (2004)[1] mandates that students with a disability must have transition goals included in their Individualized Education Program (IEP)[2,3] no later than the school year they will be 16. Parental participation in this process is the most effective way to ensure that the IEP accurately reflects the student's goals. It is also essential that the teenager attend all meetings regarding his future. The Transition Plan should be designed to explore the student's dreams, wishes, and goals.

Families of teenagers with special needs may want to request a special "transition meeting" separate from the IEP process. This transition meeting should elicit a wide range of information about the teenager and not be limited to school goals. Information regarding financial support, legal concerns, and long-term housing should be discussed. At this meeting families can gather essential information so they can begin to research the most appropriate adult service options for the teen. Emphasis should be placed on involving the student and finding out what he enjoys, is good at, wants to learn more about, as well as specific steps he will need to take to become more independent. Parents, school staff who work with the student, and agency personnel who are or will become involved may attend this meeting in order to help the student explore as many of his dreams as is practical.

Some of the information from the transition meeting may be used to develop the Transition Plan for the student's IEP. It may also be useful to develop a specific list of next steps, including who is responsible and a timeframe in which the information will be gathered. For example, if one of the student's goals is to learn to drive there are many parts of this goal that he and the team need to get information about to determine if this is achievable. The student could go on the Department of Motor Vehicles (DMV) website to find out the requirements for obtaining a driver's license in his state and county. School personnel can explore options for special education driver's training while agency staff can look into other types of driver training programs. Parents may assist the teen by bringing him to the DMV and helping him complete the necessary paperwork.

While these activities may not translate directly into IEP goals, there are certainly many IEP and transition goals that support these activities. The student's ability to access information about the DMV will require him to use computer skills, and reading skills. He will need to advocate for himself to get the information from the rest of the team. As he gathers information he will use organizational skills to keep track of it and decision-making skills to figure out the next steps based on the feedback he receives. This example highlights how the student can be an active participant in his future and pursue his dream of learning to drive. Actively participating in this process allows the teen to more realistically assess his own abilities as they relate to his stated goal. The teen may learn that driving is not a reasonable short-term goal but he will gain this knowledge himself by undertaking the steps in the process.

Part of the Transition Plan should include specific steps that will be put in place to assess the student's skills and identify areas that need to be improved in order for him to achieve his goals.

The educational team may need to find ways to make programmatic changes that support the new goals. The fact that a particular activity has not been done in the past does not mean it can't be done if it is determined to be essential to meet a documented need for the teenager to access adult life. Optimally, parents and school personnel work cooperatively with the student and incorporate activities and methods to ensure that his goals are thoroughly explored. This process needs to include opportunities for the student to re-define his goals as his understanding of his skills and the demands of the real world come together. The following example highlights how this process can work:

> Brian and his parents are hoping that he will be able to find a job that parallels his interest in computers. Although Brian reads below grade level, his parents have hired private tutors to work with him at home to develop competencies in keyboarding and accessing websites. Prior to Brian's IEP meeting with the Committee on Special Education, Brian's parents requested a meeting with his teacher to discuss ways of incorporating Brian's dreams into his school program. While Brian's teacher assured his parents that all of the children in her class are receiving computer training at the learning center twice a week, Brian's parents requested that he focus on specific skills when he is in the learning center, such as improving his keyboarding speed and accuracy as well as adding proof reading, fact checking, and an introduction to programs commonly used in business.
>
> In addition, Brian's parents recognize that to significantly increase Brian's speed and accuracy he will need to work on his computer skills more than twice a week. Therefore, they requested that the IEP specify that Brian will participate at the learning center a minimum of five times a week. With his teacher they re-wrote goals that incorporated the exploration of specific skills that they believe Brian will need in order to pursue his career goal.

Applying the school's resources in this manner allows Brian the opportunity to focus on the development of basic competencies for the career he wishes to enter. In addition, Brian would benefit from the opportunity to visit actual worksites where jobs of the type he is interested in are performed. All of these experiences will help Brian make an informed choice about his future. Brian's IEP was re-written to include goals that provide opportunities for meaningful exploration and skill building that could lead to Brian's stated future career goal or that will give him the information he needs to re-think his goal should it prove untenable.

Assessment

Most teenagers do not have a clear idea of a career goal. One of the ways to explore career interests is through the completion of a Level I Assessment. Parents, students, and teachers separately complete a questionnaire that is designed to help them focus on long-term adult goals. This questionnaire explores areas of interest that can be used to develop the Transition Plan. Level I Assessments are reviewed and updated annually and as such provide information for refining the IEP and transition goals.

When more detailed information is needed, the IEP team may request that the teenager participate in a Level II Assessment. A Level II Assessment incorporates a battery of standardized tests that are given by a trained professional such as a vocational rehabilitation counselor. These tests are designed to explore the teenager's career interests, aptitudes, and skills along with their learning style and the amount of support they are likely to need to pursue particular career choices. The standardized tests used in a Level II Assessment provide objective feedback as to a student's skills and aptitudes as compared to his peer group. This information can be useful for refining career goals. Often the Level II Assessment report will recommend possible sources for additional training and areas for further skill development that the student will need to focus on while still in school.

Some teenagers with special needs do not perform well in testing situations. In these cases, a Level III Assessment may be the most meaningful way of determining a student's work potential. Level III is a situational assessment. This means the student is encouraged to try out various types of work in real work settings with the support and supervision they need. Participating in Level III Assessments allows the student the opportunity for hands-on work experiences so they can increase their understanding of the expectations of different kinds of work. These may be referred to as work internships. The educational and/or vocational staff who work with the student assess the student's response to each work setting. Various aspects of work abilities can be explored in this manner including, but not limited to: work rate and accuracy, stamina, ability to focus in different environments, response to social demands on the job, and the ability to work as part of a team.

Vocational staff will utilize the Level III Assessments to review with the student and his family areas of strength as well as areas that they will need to improve if competitive employment is the goal. Internships can then be developed that address the student's demonstrated strengths and interests and when possible minimize areas of deficit. Continual reassessment will optimally lead to a greater understanding of realistic post-secondary outcomes.

Volunteer and paid employment

Volunteer and/or part-time paid employment is another avenue teens can take to identify career goals. Most volunteer opportunities can be obtained after the age of 14. Depending on the community, there may be a few paid positions available to 14- and 15-year-olds, but most employers require paid employees to be 16, 17, or even 18 for some positions. It cannot be over-emphasized that participation in volunteer or paid employment will be a maturing experience for a teenager.

While the teenager with special needs can be expected to require greater assistance with this process, his challenges should not preclude him from being a contributing member of his community. Parents may need to investigate the requirements for various volunteer positions or entry-level jobs and then inquire as to what resources the school can provide to support the teenager's efforts. The school guidance or vocational counselor may assist a student with the process of finding and obtaining appropriate work opportunities.

There are several models of support that will facilitate success at work or when a teen is volunteering. Sometimes, a "natural support" co-worker[8] can be identified. This is another employee or student who can lend a helping hand to the employee with special needs, if needed. There may also be opportunities to participate in a mentoring program in which a knowledgeable staff member or community worker provides feedback and strategies for the new worker to be successful.

For teenagers who require more significant supports, the use of a job coach[6] can make all the difference. Job coaches are para-professionals who work for either the school system or a community agency. Job coaches provide hands-on/on-site support and training to an employee with special needs while they are learning the skills and social competencies for success on the job. Working with a job coach falls under the category of "Supported Employment."[9] The idea is to provide intensive support that gradually decreases as the student demonstrates the ability to handle the job on his own. Job coaches will gradually "fade,"[7] spending less time with the employee as he acquires the skills necessary to do the job.

If the teen has taken technical courses, the teachers of these classes should be able to provide a wealth of information regarding their field and possible avenues of entry. A note of caution –

participating in a technical class does not imply mastery of even entry-level requirements needed to secure employment in the field. A frank conversation with the teacher regarding the teen's aptitude for this type of work can help identify which skills the teenager has consistently demonstrated as well as areas that require additional training or practice. This can give the parent and teenager a better idea of the teen's readiness for a paid position.

Volunteer experiences are often more readily available and may provide the teen with an opportunity to develop his altruistic interests and learn new skills. While helping others, volunteer positions may also provide opportunities for the teenager to acquire new skills and give structure to his schedule. Participating in volunteer work that brings the student into contact with people who are less fortunate than he can be a sensitizing and maturing experience. The recognition that he is needed to accomplish certain activities will more than likely enhance the teen's self-esteem. Being part of a team that helps others or supporting a cause he believes in may provide a venue for him to see himself in a whole new way.

Independence in the community

Before a teenager or young adult accesses the community independently they must consistently demonstrate an understanding of personal safety. Whether holding down a job, doing volunteer work, or frequenting community businesses on his own, the young adult must know how to keep himself physically safe. In addition, consistently demonstrating safe pedestrian skills is essential. When possible the teenager needs to learn how to cross streets of varying complexity, i.e. single lane streets/at a stop sign/using street lights, etc. Parents will want to ensure that the teenager is aware of possible dangers when they use the community as well as the best methods to obtain assistance if needed.

While it may be easiest and most reassuring for parents to hold the child's hand when crossing streets and parking lots, relying on physical contact is not a long-term solution. Parents need to take the time to teach safety awareness rather than relying on physical methods to control the child as they become a teenager. Physical contact may be inappropriate beyond a certain chronological age, plus the child is likely to someday be bigger and stronger than the parent, making reliance on physical methods of control untenable.

In many cases, teenagers will benefit from the opportunity to learn how to use public transportation. Safe use of public buses, trains, and even taxi cabs will allow the teenager access to more community activities and additional avenues for employment as well as social experiences. People with special needs may be eligible for half fare cards that will allow them access to public transportation for half the typical cost. Half fare cards can be obtained through the transit system and will require specific documentation.

Some communities have a para-transit system that provides people who are unable to ride the public bus system with door-to-door transportation. This generally costs more than the public bus but less than cab service. Para-transit systems require the completion of an application that documents the reasons why the person cannot ride the public bus system. (The fact that no public bus service is available in the area is not considered a valid reason for eligibility for para-transit service.)

Some special education students may be interested in learning to drive. Each state designates the ages and restrictions for driving privileges. Information regarding obtaining a driver's license is available from your state's DMV office. Many states require a potential driver under a certain age to obtain a learner's permit prior to participation in driver's training. In order to obtain a learner's permit, the student must achieve a certain score on a multiple choice test based on the driver's manual that is available from the DMV or on-line. Special accommodations may be utilized to take this test such as having a "reader."[10] Special accommodations must be scheduled in advance with the DMV.

If the school district offers driver's education to the general population they are required to offer the special education student this opportunity as well. Special education students may participate in a special evaluation prior to starting driver's training classes. This evaluation should assess the student's eye–hand coordination, eye–foot reaction, and vision under differing light conditions. Balance and spatial orientation will also be assessed. This should be a comprehensive evaluation that is usually designed by an occupational therapist. The evaluation will result in a report that has three possible recommendations. First, it may recommend participation in regular driver's education. In New York State Drivers' Education training, for general education students, requires a minimum 24 hours of classroom instruction, 18 hours of driving observation and 6 hours behind the wheel. Second, it may recommend a special education driver's education course. This is one-to-one driver's training in which the student is the only driver for the entire course. Third, it may not recommend driver's education at this time, and explain the reasons it is not recommended. The IEP team should be notified prior to the annual review regarding the teen's interest in driver's training.

Further reading and useful resources

Department of Motor Vehicles – www.dmv.org

Hughes, C. and Carter, E. (2000) *The Transition Handbook Strategies High School Teachers Use that Work!* Baltimore, MD: Paul H. Brooks.

Marquette, J. (2007) *Independence Bound and Becoming Remarkably Able: Walking the Path to Independence and Beyond.* Louisville, KY: Jackie Marquette. Available at www.independencebound.com

National Center on Secondary Education and Transition – Parent Brief (2005) *Age of Majority: Preparing Your Child for Making Good Choices.* Minneapolis, MN: University of Minnesota, Center for Community Integration. Available at www.ncset.org/publications

National Center on Secondary Education and Transition – Parent Brief (2005) *Self-determination for Middle and High School Students.* Minneapolis, MN: University of Minnesota, Center for Community Integration. Available at www.ncset.org/topics

Organization for Autism Research (OAR) (2007) *Life Journey Through Autism: A Guide for Transition to Adulthood.* Silver Springs, MD: Danya International, Inc. Available at www.danya.com

Rhode Island Parent Information Network (2005) *Here's to Your Student's Future! A Parent's Guide to Transition Planning.* Available at www.ripin.org

Wehman, P. (2006) *Life Beyond the Classroom: Transition Strategies for Young People with Disabilities, 4th edition.* Baltimore, MD: Paul H. Brookes Publishing Company.

6

Person Centered Planning – Putting the Student First!

As the young adult with special needs prepares to leave the familiarity of the school system they need to be sure not to leave behind the wealth of information and expertise that has been gathered with and about them during their years in school. Families are most often encouraged to focus on accessing new services from programs and systems that are designed for adults with disabilities. Adult programs may take a specific role providing one type of service and may have limited connections with other agencies that are also working with the young adult. In addition, adult services personnel often have large caseloads that limit the amount of time and attention they can give to any one person with whom they work.

This leaves the family and the young adult with the responsibility of providing all of the background information as well as an explanation of the young adult's unique needs and desires. This information needs to be targeted to the specific service each adult agency is going to provide. For example, an application for social security benefits will require financial and legal information as well as the results of any standardized testing, psychological and/or psychiatric reports, and medical information. Adult day programs will want more detailed information regarding the day-to-day functioning and level of support needed by the young adult. College programs will need academic information and test scores. While all of this information is readily available to families at their request prior to the young adult exiting school, it can become much more difficult to access once they have graduated. The family and the young adult are legally responsible for providing whatever information is requested to any of the adult service programs in which they wish to participate.

Participation in Person Centered Planning (PCP),[11] sometimes called Personal Futures Planning or Essential Lifestyle Planning, is a wonderful process by which families and adults with special needs may collect information from the perspective of the various people who are in his life. A PCP will organize this information and use it to develop a plan of action that is a series of action steps. Each person who contributes to the PCP should leave the meeting with a deeper understanding of the person with special needs and a clearer idea of how they will assist with the exploration of his goals.

Families who have the opportunity to participate in a Person Centered Planning meeting will gain from the expertise shared by the school staff. When adult service providers are able to attend the PCP meeting there is a natural exchange of information that benefits the young adult during his transition. The PCP report will include a summary of all of the information that has been gathered from the educational team. Families can then choose to share this report with adult service program staff during the young adult's initial entry into these services. Optimally a PCP will be repeated as the needs and interests of the young adult change.

Nuts and bolts of the process

Person Centered Planning is often offered through adult service agencies but it may be available within the school setting even if in a modified form. When PCPs are done outside of the school setting a group of supportive friends and relatives may partici-pate in the process. This group of people should represent differ-ent facets of the person's life. The team may work together over a period of years to assist a person with a disability and his family with ongoing support as he matures.

Within the school setting a PCP may be done with all of the staff who work closely with the student as well as any other sup-portive people the family wishes to invite. Members of the Indi-vidualized Education Program (IEP)[3] or Committee on Special Education (CSE)[12] team may be involved as well as any person-nel from outside agencies, such as Service Coordinators,[13] job coaches[6] etc. A PCP meeting does not replace the IEP meeting; however, the information that is gathered should be useful when writing IEP goals and transition plans.

Families will want to select a facilitator who has been trained in the philosophy and methods involved in Person Centered Planning. The facilitator should also have knowledge of the student and the family and access to the professional team who work most closely with them. The facilitator may be responsible for organizing the meeting and for listening and accurately interpreting the student's strengths, wishes, and goals as well as any possible obstacles, and steps needed to meet those goals. There should also be a recorder who assumes responsibility for writing down everything that is shared during the meeting and then sees that the information is typed and distributed to everyone who attended.

Two of the most significant differences between a PCP and the IEP meeting are that the PCP is designed to look at the whole person across different environments and learn about his skills in different situations. Also, in a PCP every person's input is equally sought and acknowledged. There is no hierarchy for decision-making. The meeting focuses exclusively on the person the meeting is for. Each team member is equally welcome to par-ticipate by sharing information about the student/teenager they know.

The philosophy behind the tool

A PCP meeting explores the whole person. Gathering people from various parts of the teen's life should allow for a view into how he responds in different environments and under a variety of conditions. PCP meetings are based on the student's strengths, abilities, interests, and dreams. PCP meetings are ability-focused; the student's strengths are explored along with the supports they need to address any areas of challenge.

A PCP meeting creates an opportunity for each participant to discuss and highlight the student's positive qualities, strengths, and desires. This helps draw a more holistic picture and a clearer direction for goal setting. It also helps the family and school staff find common ground regarding the student's future plans. As a result of the meeting they will have the opportunity to develop a shared plan for how best to proceed on the student's behalf.

An essential component of the PCP meeting is for the young adult not only to be present but an active participant to whatever extent they are able. While it can certainly be an overwhelming experience to be required to sit with the team you work with and listen to their perspectives about you, the PCP meeting is a unique opportunity for the young adult to hear from people who know him well, how they see him, and what their expectations are for him. Even more important, the PCP meeting is an opportunity for the young adult to explore his own goals and dreams with people who are interested in helping him realize those goals.

Optimally, the young adult with a disability has had many opportunities during his annual IEP meetings to participate as a part of a team and discuss his goals. Students need to be prepared for this experience so they can feel comfortable expressing themselves and to understand the need to use the meeting for its intended purpose, that is, to identify educational goals that will assist the student in his exploration of his future. Attendance at

IEP meetings is a wonderful opportunity for a teenager to develop critical self-advocacy skills that they will need throughout their adult life.

It is not uncommon for a teenager to select a goal that the team believes is inconsistent with his actual abilities. The team needs to work with the teen and help him explore his goals as they relate to his aptitudes and abilities. They need to find methods and experiences that will allow the teen to learn about himself and to assess his abilities. However, the critical work necessary for a seamless transition cannot occur if the teen is not included in the process of determining his unique wishes, goals, and dreams. The following example demonstrates the use of a PCP in the school setting.

> *Ryan is a student with significant challenges. He is selectively mute, has a unique posture, and limited gross motor skills. He is very shy and has trouble making eye contact. Most of the staff that work closest with Ryan believed that he would be best served by participation in a full-time day program after graduation from school. However, his mother knew that he had more to offer; she visualized him having a part-time job.*
>
> *During the PCP meeting the job developer learned many new things about Ryan. She learned that Ryan loved classical music and books. She discovered that he had alphabetizing skills. She also found out just how great Ryan's own desire was to get a job after he left school. Utilizing that motivation, the job developer began working intensively with Ryan to increase his voice volume, improve eye contact, and improve his productivity at his volunteer worksite, a local library. Ryan also received ongoing support for the development of these skills from every member of his team, including his special education teacher, speech pathologist, and occupational therapist.*

His mother also increased the amount of time and number of opportunities Ryan spent participating in the community. Ryan was beginning to thrive under the light of all of this positive attention that focused on building his skills for work. One of the staff members noticed that Ryan lived right down the block from a large bookstore. The job developer contacted the manager who asked to meet Ryan and was willing to try him out in a part-time, unpaid internship.

During the next few months Ryan had the opportunity to work at the bookstore with the assistance of a one-on-one-job coach. The manager was willing to explore the parameters of Ryan's limitations and with the job coach they carved out a specific job responsibility that Ryan was able to perform. Ryan was in charge of organizing and alphabetizing one floor-to-ceiling wall of books that extended the entire length of the store. By the time Ryan reached the end of the wall it was time to go back to the beginning and start over. The repetition of this job, along with the ongoing support of his co-workers and job coach, gradually helped Ryan feel more comfortable and confident in the job.

Ryan enjoyed the quiet music that played in the background and loved working with books. However, he continued to have challenges when approached by a customer; most often he ignored their requests for assistance. The job coach and speech teacher continued to work with Ryan practicing "scripts" of responses he could use when dealing with a customer. Ryan was occasionally able to respond audibly. He learned to direct customers to the bathrooms or to get another employee who could help with other types of questions.

As a result of the PCP, the staff working with Ryan gained a clearer understanding of his strengths and goals. Ryan continued to work at this job after graduation.

The National Center on Secondary Education and Transition (2004) states:

> At its best, the person-centered planning process can strengthen the transition to post-school activities by:
> - enhancing the quality of assessment and planning activities for both the school transition services and adult service agencies serving youth with disabilities
> - fostering positive working relationships between professionals and families
> - providing a way for educators and case managers from other agencies to better coordinate their services
> - connecting families to adult service agencies before a student leaves school
> - helping ensure that services support the youth's goals and lead to desired outcomes
> - helping identify and cultivate natural supports in the community.

Families can find out more about Person Centered Planning services from the transition team at school or the adult service provider. The State Office of Developmental Disabilities or Vocational Rehabilitation Services Office may be able to direct a parent to a trained facilitator who can provide the expertise needed to conduct this type of meeting.

Further reading and useful resources

Beach Center on Families and Disabilities, articles on Person-Centered Planning – www.beachcenter.org

Essential Lifestyle Planning – www.allenshea.com

MAPS: McGill Action Planning System for Making Action Plans – http://challengingbehavior.fmhi.usf.edu

O'Brien, J., Forest, M., Snow, J. and Hasbury, D. (1989) *Action for Inclusion.* Canada: Frontier College Press.

Oregon Department of Education Transition (2007) *Key Provisions in Secondary Transition for Students with Disabilities.* Available at www.ode.state.or.us/gradelevel

Person Centered Planning: Maps and Paths to the Future –
www.ttac.odu.edu/Articles/person.html

www.ncset.org/publications/viewdesc.asp?id=1431

US Department of Education (2000) *A Guide to the Individualized Education Program.* Available at
www.ed.gov/parents/needs/speced/iepguide/index.html

PART II

The School Bus Doesn't
Stop Here Any More

7

High School Graduation,
Then What...?

The Individuals with Disabilities Education Act (Section 618)[1] allows for all special education students to extend their high school experience beyond the typical four years until they have completed all of the requirements for graduation up till the school year they are 21 years old. In some instances, the school district may continue to support the student's educational program in order for him to meet his written transition goals as well as those needed to attain a local high school diploma. Although extending high school can be emotionally charged for the student and his family, consideration of the young adult's needs as well as the opportunities the school district can provide should be carefully explored. Parents may have to do some independent research to find other types of programs outside of the high school setting that could offer more effective transitional support for the student who is older than a typical high school student. These programs may be paid for by the school district. The guidance or vocational counselor or a Service Coordinator[12] can be helpful in identifying programs outside of the high school setting as well as appropriate funding sources. The school district can be asked to fund identified transition needs and support services as long as the student has not met all of the requirements for a high school diploma.

It is critical that the family and the student begin exploring program options with the Individualized Education Program (IEP)[3] team prior to the expected year of graduation. Steve Riggio, a parent of a young adult with special needs, was quoted by Rubin and Aduroja (2005) in the Chicago Tribune as saying: "The availability of programs after high school was like going from a cruise ship to a dinghy." School district personnel may genuinely need additional time to navigate the school system effectively and identify avenues for support, particularly for a program they have never provided before. If the student formally graduates, they are no longer eligible for school district funding and must rely on adult service funding, which is generally significantly less than district supports. Some school district personnel have found ways to allow the special education student to "walk" with their graduating class but not officially graduate. The student may then attend an appropriate transition program under the auspices of the school district. Again, parents are urged to assess carefully whether the many resources of the local school district would best support the young adult's transition programming beyond the typical four years and possibly until June of the school year the student is 21.

Parents are advised to investigate all appropriate adult programs and services, whether they are school district sanctioned, private pay, or funded through Medicaid, in order to identify which will best serve the young adult's needs. Parents will want to familiarize themselves with the goals and structure of the program, as well as the number and types of support staff. Optimally, the parents and the young adult, when possible, have developed a clear understanding of the types of support and training he needs to participate in his desired goals. This information will be crucial when choosing the best next step. Whether a student is planning on attending college, a training program, or an adult service day program, the parent continues to be the young adult's best advocate, though the form their advocacy takes may shift to assisting the young adult to speak up for himself when appropriate.

Self-determination and self-advocacy

Throughout this book parents are urged to support the young adult in the process of selecting goals that will help determine his future. They are encouraged to include the child, teen, and young adult in decision-making, problem-solving and goal setting activities from early childhood into adult life. These recommendations are based on the premise that people need many opportunities to develop a sense of self. People need supportive opportunities to make decisions in order to develop self-advocacy skills. Exercising self-advocacy skills will improve the young adult's chance of achieving a positive transition outcome; that is to say, a satisfying and productive adult life.

Current research supports the concept that effective self-advocacy skills enhance the young adult's success at meeting his goals (Wehman 2006). When given opportunities to make meaningful choices, a person can develop a sense of empowerment that impacts across many different areas of his life. Self-determination skills help one to maintain control of emotions, teach responsibility, and allow a person to learn that their actions have consequences.

Wehman (2006) recommends professionals adopt methods that allow the student opportunities to learn self-determination skills. Encouraging students to make choices and to deal with the consequences of those decisions may require staff to learn new ways of supporting students' goals. Hughes and Carter (2000) state:

> Self-determination is as much about changing our behavior as it is about changing our students' behavior. It's time to let students learn to make their own decisions and choices, learn from their own successes and mistakes, and try new experiences when the opportunity comes

along. It's time for us to learn how to support students in making and acting on their own decisions, rather than making those decisions for them. (p.185)

While limited opportunities for decision-making are common in the school setting, it can also be difficult for parents to step back and allow the young adult to learn to manage his personal life. Parents need to find ways to support the young adult's emerging self-advocacy skills. Adult living requires the ability to make decisions in order to advocate effectively for one's self. People with special needs must have opportunities to develop skills that will allow them to live as independently as they are able to when they transition out of the school system. Both educators and parents may be equally culpable in trying to protect the young adult; these attitudes may increase the burden of his disability rather than prepare him for effective ways to deal with adult life.

College programs

In order to be accepted into college all students must meet the requirements for admission. However, there is a wide range of support services available for a student with an identified disability who is planning on attending college. Currently, a high school diploma or a General Education Diploma (GED)[14] are the only types of diplomas that are recognized for acceptance into a traditional college program. An IEP diploma does not meet this requirement.

Although a student with a 504 Plan[15] will continue to receive protection from discrimination, in college the student is responsible for seeking out the support he needs. The student must research and follow the college's procedures to obtain accommodations and provide documentation that legitimizes his request. The student who continues to require accommodations for learning must be prepared to discuss these accommodations with each of his professors. College programs do not identify a student with a disability and inform the course instructor of the student's special needs. The student is responsible for advocating for himself at college.

This illustrates some of the changes that students need to prepare for as they transition from high school. At the same time parents need to make some significant adjustments. Parents of young adults must move into a mentor or advisor role rather than that of direct advocate for the college student's services. For this to be an effective shift, parents must maintain open communication with the young adult. Although it is difficult, parents may need to allow the young adult to make mistakes so they can learn from them. In the long run it is not in anyone's best interests for the parent to take over and solve the young adult's problems. If the parent feels they must act, their first response needs to be that of advisor to the young adult. Parents need to learn how to provide helpful information that the young adult can then choose to act on in his own behalf.

It is strongly recommended that students and their families tour all campuses under consideration, paying particular attention to the programs offered through the office for students with special needs. The array of support services varies widely at different colleges. Services such as tutoring, counseling, small group remedial classes, and readers[10] are just a few of the types of assistance a student may find on a particular campus. Some support services are included in the tuition and fees but most will entail an additional cost. It is essential that the student find a program that will support their unique needs. However, it is equally important that they utilize the services once they are on campus.

Some families feel that the teenager has struggled under the "stigma" of the disability label through high school and that they should be allowed to make a fresh start in college. This is a decision that requires careful examination and extreme caution. College attendance removes all of the support and structure that high school offers. Even students who actively rebelled against the structure of high school may find themselves at a loss as to how best to use their time in college.

College schedules are totally different from high school. College classes are not scheduled from 7am to 2pm Monday through Friday, but are offered at varying times and days. There is the expectation that the college student is utilizing their out of class time to further their understanding and knowledge of the subject matter. The increased demands on the student's organizational skills, time management, and self-advocacy can be challenging for all students but the student with special needs can be particularly vulnerable in these areas.

The transition to college life, with its implicit additional requirements for self-regulation, increased pace, and academic expectations, presents even the most able high school students with enormous new challenges. Often, students and families do not recognize the amount of support that students with special needs are given informally by their teachers, support staff, and classmates while in high school. In addition, the structure and support that has developed at home may have played a critical role in enabling this child to meet the requirements for high school graduation.

It is not uncommon for the new college student either to decide he does not need the assistance of the office of special services or just not to make the time to avail himself of this support. Support program staff will not generally "find" a student who does not show up for an appointment. Unfortunately, when the student is unwilling to seek the assistance they need they may find they cannot keep up with the college workload. Parents will have no way of knowing how the student is doing unless the student chooses to share this information. It is critical to remember that post-secondary programs are not mandatory. Students cannot be required to attend; they must want to.

Self-assessment skills are often not well developed in young adults, yet these will be needed in order to ascertain whether or not additional help should be sought out. Establishing an ongoing relationship with the special needs program staff can provide the college student with objective feedback throughout the semester. Also, special needs office personnel can often assist the student in scheduling their classes. Advice may be sought on issues of class size and times, which professors work well with learners with special needs, and how to manage time between classes. Obtaining this "inside information" will help the student make choices that best fit his learning needs.

The WNY Collegiate Consortium of Disability Advocates (2006) states:

> The most important concept to grasp is that the student with a disability needs *all* the same competencies as any other college student *plus* whatever special skills or strategies are needed to cope with his disability. It is better to start acquiring skills in an environment he knows well (i.e. high school) rather than to wait until he arrives on the college campus. Going to a college comfortable with oneself and one's needs can make the difference between success and failure. (p.1)

This highlights the need for the transitioning student to have the opportunity to access information and develop a clear understanding about his unique challenges and the strategies that allow him to be successful before he exits the school system.

It is important for the student with special needs who transitions to a college program to have a clear understanding of the nature of his disability and the types of accommodations he will require. It is not unusual for parents and students to decide that the "issues" the teenager had in high school were specific to that setting. They may be convinced that the child will outgrow his challenges when presented with the opportunities that a college program has to offer. They may feel there is no need to bring the information and expertise from the high school setting with him to college. While this may be the case at times, most students with special needs continue to require extra supports to perform successfully in the college setting. Specific, detailed information regarding accessing college programs is available from the George Washington University website (see Useful resources for more details).

Useful resources

Broatch, L. (2005) *Transition to Adulthood: Focusing on Life after High School*, Schwab Learning. Available at www.schwablearning.org/articles.aspx?r=970

General Education Development Testing Service, American Council on Education. Available at www.acenet.edu/am/template.cfm?section=GEDTS

George Washington University HEATH Resource Center Online Clearinghouse on Postsecondary Education for Individuals with Disabilities (2006) *Guidance and Career Counselors' Toolkit.* Available at www.heath.gwu.edu/node/15#attachments

Ken-Crest Centers (2005) *Transition Map: Where Do We Go From Here?* Available at www.transitionmap.org

National Center on Secondary Education and Transition – Parent Brief (2005) *Age of Majority: Preparing Your Child for Making Good Choices.* Minneapolis, MN: University of Minnesota, Center for Community Integration. Available at www.ncset.org/publications/viewdesc.asp?id=318

Sevier County Special Education (2007) *IEPs vs. 504 Plans.* Available at www.slc.sevier.org/iepv504.htm

US Department of Education, Office of Civil Rights (2002) *Students with Disabilities Preparing for the Postsecondary Education: Know Your Rights and Responsibilities.* Available at www.ed.gov/about/offices/list/ocr/transition.htm

8

Alphabet Soup – Programs and Services for Adults

When the young adult reaches the end of their educational program, parental advocacy will again be critical. Unlike special education services, *there is no law that mandates adult services or programs*. Since the child's entry into the school system, parents have learned to negotiate various aspects of his Individualized Education Program (IEP)[3]. As he transitions from the school system, a whole new world of opportunity must be explored in order for the young adult to have access to the supports that will allow him to lead a productive and safe adult life.

Although transitioning to adult services is a new challenge for the young adult with special needs and his family, there are programs and services that are designed to help. The following is an overview of the various types of programs, including: financial supports, work and day program options, residential life, and recreational opportunities. This is not a comprehensive list but rather an introduction to services with information a parent can use to research similar programming in their community. Websites and other resources are included at the end of this chapter for families to learn more about a specific type of program or agency.

Preparing for new opportunities

During the last few years of school, adult service program providers may assume a larger role in the student's educational plan in a variety of ways, including but not limited to: finding and supervising volunteer and/or paid internships, providing opportunities for job specific training programs, referral information and assistance with application completion, and (perhaps most critically) providing the knowledge and understanding of specific program requirements and their relevance to this particular student's needs. Parents may have to take an active role to inform and encourage the educational team to incorporate the expertise of the adult program providers into the transition plan.

Adult service programs will place a much greater emphasis on the young adult's preferences, skills, and abilities than may be found in many school programs. Active participation by the young adult in all meetings related to their programming is an expected and usual practice. Therefore, including the student in his school-based meetings is an important step to prepare him for participation in these adult meetings as well. Professionals who have a rapport with the student and/or the student's family will want to prepare the student for the meeting. Discussing who will attend and what will be discussed, as well as eliciting the student's input and ideas that he can later share in the meeting, should be helpful.

Generally, all adult service meetings including applying for Social Security, vocational services, college programs, and intakes to adult agencies will focus on the adult with special needs. He will be expected to answer questions to the best of his ability. He may be asked to describe his disability and explain the impact it has on different areas of his life. This question can confuse and surprise the young adult unless he has had the advantage of open and supportive discussions regarding his particular learning style and abilities, as well as areas of ongoing challenges, with his family and support team.

While most professionals want to project the best possible outcome for the children they work with, it is essential that they share with the student and his family the information they need to describe the student's challenges in functional language that can be understood by the student and other adults who do not work in the field. This practical information allows families to understand the needs of the child and to investigate more effectively and advocate for methods to overcome and/or work with challenges. Providing this information may help alleviate some of the fear and confusion that can hinder the parents' ability to make realistic plans. When people do not have a clear understanding of the nature and impact of a child's disability on his day-to-day life and his future, they won't know which adult programs and services the young adult may require or even whether or not he will need this type of support.

The young adult who learns how to discuss his challenges, the supports that help him, his goals, and his dreams, has the skills he needs to advocate effectively for himself. This information will help ensure that the services that are offered are ones that will meet his unique needs. The family and the professionals who work closely with the student are in the best position to assist him to accurately and succinctly explain his support needs to others in language that he understands. This information is the basis for the development of self-advocacy skills. As such, this skill is useful for students of all functioning levels regardless of expected adult outcomes. Students anticipating attending college, in particular, need to develop the ability to advocate for themselves. But even young adults with more significant challenges will benefit from being able to make choices, to say "no," and to stand up for themselves.

Ongoing discussions throughout the teen years, regarding the expertise they are acquiring and the supports they need to build on these new skills, will serve the young adult well in adult life. Simple functional language that refrains from the use of jargon and diagnoses is the most effective way to ensure clarity and understanding. Phrases such as:

- "I take a longer time to learn new things"
- "Sometimes I can be easily upset"
- "I need time to adjust to changes"
- "I don't like loud noises"

are just a few examples of functional, understandable language that describes a challenge.

Equally important are phrases that outline methods the teenager has or is learning to compensate for these challenges. These may include:

- "I need directions written down for me"
- "I only remember two directions at a time"
- "I like routines and schedules"
- "I walk around by myself to calm down"
- "I hear better when I stand on your right side".

These simple statements provide practical information and suggest specific methods of support the young adult needs. Identifying and practicing brief appropriate statements of this type is recommended to prepare the young adult to deal with the world of adult programs as well as the general public.

While there are many different kinds of support opportunities available to students who are exiting the educational system, parents may become overwhelmed by the variety of adult services and at the same time frustrated by the lack of programming that appears to best fit the needs of the young adult. It is essential for families to gather as much information as possible

9

Financial Support

When possible, parents may set aside money during their children's lives to help offset the cost of college or other major life purchases such as home ownership. While a child with a disability is still young there is hope that their challenges are truly developmental in nature and they will mature into a capable and independent adult. However, if a child has a significant disability he may continue to need extra support throughout his life. As the family comes to terms with this reality they may feel the need to increase the financial support they set aside for the child with special needs. For those adults who continue to require special supports in order to pursue a meaningful life, having money in their name can actually impede their access to government programs and services that could provide supports throughout their lifetime. In fact, most government funded adult programs do not allow for a private pay option.

Although most parents want to see that the child with special needs is taken care of, in many cases families put off this essential task. The New York State Developmental Disabilities Guide (2006) cites three of the most common reasons why families don't plan:

1. fear of our own mortality

2. fear of being unfair to our family members with disabilities

3.   anxiety over selecting/hiring an attorney.[17]

Parents are urged to discuss their concerns with the appropriate professionals so they can move forward and develop a long-term plan that addresses the needs of the child.

The Rhode Island Parent Information Network (2005) suggests that parents consider the following before starting this process:

- How independent is my son or daughter?

- Can my son or daughter earn a living and handle his or her own finances?

- Where does he or she want to live?

- What are my financial resources now (savings, life insurance, trust funds)?

- What do I think my financial resources will be over the next ten years?

- Will my son or daughter need government benefits such as Supplemental Security Income (SSI), subsidized housing, a personal care attendant, or Medicaid?

- How can I plan my estate to protect those benefits?

- Will a family member be designated to care for my son or daughter?

- Will my son or daughter need a guardian or conservator?

A Supplemental Needs Trust[17] will allow the adult with special needs access to appropriate government programs. Parents are urged to discuss these concerns with an "elder-lawyer or estate planning attorney" who has experience of planning for adult children with disabilities. An attorney with this expertise can

advise parents on the specific legal requirements that will assist the child throughout his lifetime.

Government funded support services

Adults with a disability that limit their ability to perform an essential life function such as earning a living may be eligible for government funding through several different avenues. Families of children who receive special education services are urged to explore government funded resources as part of the young adult's transition process. While the need for special education support services does not guarantee government sponsored financial assistance, parents should research the appropriate program that might best meet the young adult's needs as they leave the school system.

The Social Security Administration (SSA) administers both the Supplemental Security Income (SSI) and Social Security Disability Insurance (SSDI). Although each of these programs can be a source of monthly income, eligibility requirements are quite different. The SSA determines eligibility. Although inclusion in special education services does not in any way ensure social security eligibility, parents are urged to contact SSA if the young adult is receiving special education services. Eligibility can only be determined through participation in the intake process.

To initiate this process the SSA should be contacted to set up an appointment for the parent and the young adult when the teenager turns 18. Again – all meetings for adult service programming must include the young adult. Even if the family was denied benefits in the past, the parent should again start the process to determine if the young adult with a disability is now eligible for benefits. At age 18 the decision regarding benefits eligibility is based on the young adult's financial assets alone – excluding family income. However, all monies that are in the young adult's name are included in this determination. The specific financial requirements are available by calling the 1-800-772-1213 (toll-free) number or by contacting the local Independent Living Center.

Once again, parents may need to speak up for the young adult whose disability impacts on his ability to become self-supporting. An example of one parent's initial struggle to access financial support for his son follows:

Jon is an 18-year-old special education student who lives with his parents and a younger brother. Jon has no financial assets in his name. Although his parents both work they were told that Jon might be eligible for need-based SSI when he was 18. Jon's father calls the 1-800 number and is asked who his son lives with. He says his son lives at home with his parents. He is told that if he lives at home he is not eligible for SSI. Jon's father hangs up but is confused. He checks with Jon's school counselor who assures him that other students who live at home do *receive SSI. Jon's father calls again and gets a different person on the phone. He is asked to describe Jon's disability. Jon's dad explains the multiple challenges his son deals with. Jon's father is told that SSI is only for people with physical disabilities. He knows this is not true, so he asks to speak with a supervisor. He is told the supervisor is at lunch but he can call back later. Jon's father calls after lunch, answers the same set of questions with the same answers, and is given an appointment for him and his son to come in to meet with a social security representative. Jon's father supplied all of the necessary documentation and Jon was found to be eligible for SSI based on the impact his disability has on his employability and the fact that he has no personal assets.*

This story highlights the need for parents to be well informed and to persist when they are denied something for which they believe their child may be eligible. Additional assistance with this process may be needed. Some elder care attorneys are knowledgeable in benefits assistance as well as commuting agencies such as the local Independence Living Center.

SSI, unlike any of the other services for people with special needs, relies on a deficit model. That is to say, the parent must discuss the young adult's *lack* of ability and the level of support he needs to learn and manage in the community. The parent must focus on the negative impact the disability has on the young adult's ability to secure "Substantial Gainful Employment."[18] A young adult working in a part-time entry-level position with a job coach[6] should be eligible for SSI. People who meet the criteria for substantial gainful employment may start out in an entry-level job but they will more than likely receive opportunities for promotions and/or additional training.

Parents of children with disabilities who are not citizens of the United States but who are residents in the US need to apply for SSI prior to the age of 18. If the parents have worked in the country for a long enough period of time, the child may be eligible for this important support. However, once the child turns 18 his immigration status will change and he may be evaluated as an adult. Even if the child is not yet a citizen parents should call the 1-800 number and initiate the process.

Supplemental Security Income

Supplemental Security Income (SSI) is designed to provide financial support to a person with a documented disability that impacts on his employability. That is, if the young adult's disability impedes him from attaining "Substantial Gainful Employment," the ability to be self-supporting, then he may be eligible to receive a monthly SSI check. Social security law requires that the monthly stipend be used for essential life needs such as rent. If the young adult is living at home, it is recommended that the parent charge a monthly rental fee and provide a receipt for this payment. Parents need to stay apprised of the specific financial guidelines that affect eligibility for SSI.

People who receive monthly SSI payments can work. There are specific guidelines for how much an individual can make and the impact their income will have on their monthly stipend, but the general rule of thumb is for every dollar earned, the SSI check will be reduced by 50 cents.

Currently SSA does not keep monthly tabs on a recipient's income. Therefore, it is up to the family to notify SSA quarterly by registered mail regarding the individual's income and to keep the proof of this notification. At some interval, usually every three years but possibly as often as annually, the SSA will contact the family for a re-evaluation and/or notification of overpayment. In other words, the monthly check has not been changed in response to the recipient's change of monthly income.

Overpayment notification can be a frightening experience. The letter from Social Security may indicate that they are owed several thousand dollars. However, families should note that overpayments are never expected to be made at once in full but rather will be reflected by a decrease in the monthly stipend until full pay back is secured. In addition, if the family can prove that they have been notifying SSA quarterly then the "overpayment" was SSA's error and the recipient is not liable for repayments. Parents of the adult who receives SSI may wish to contact the local Independent Living Center for assistance with an overpayment notice.

While receiving the monthly SSI check can help meet basic expenses, the greater benefit is the fact that with SSI the recipient receives Medicaid benefits. Medicaid is the primary method of payment for all adult support programs. In other words, when the young adult graduates or "ages out" of the educational system, Medicaid can provide not only health benefits but also direct payment for community living opportunities, day programs, transportation, and even long-term job coaching services. In most cases, Medicaid is the only method of payment that adult support programs are set up to receive. Therefore, having Medicaid is critical in order for the adult with special needs to access the adult programs and services that they may need.

Social Security Disability Insurance

Social Security Disability Insurance (SSDI) is a program set up for people who have worked for a certain period of time and then become disabled. This rarely applies to students who are transitioning out of the school system. However, SSDI is also paid to children of adult workers with a disability and children of retired or deceased adult workers. Currently, guidelines for SSDI and employment are in fact more restrictive than the SSI guidelines but people can still hold part-time jobs and continue to receive SSDI. While SSDI monthly checks can be much higher than SSI checks, SSDI automatically comes with Medicare. While Medicare does cover a wider range of medical doctors it does not pay for adult programs. Therefore, the young adult with a significant disability will benefit more from Medicaid than Medicare benefits.

Several agencies are available to assist families with information and guidance to navigate the Social Security system as well as other forms of support. A list can be found at the end of this chapter.

Other health coverage

Most family health plans stop when a young adult leaves school or after 18 years of age. Parents are advised to contact the family's health care provider as some health care plans continue coverage for an adult with a documented disability even after they have left school and are older than the stated age of coverage.

Useful resources

The ARC – Future Planning Resources. Lists government printed booklets/pamphlets and general publications regarding estate planning, guardianship, and Personal Futures Planning. Information for lawyers and Futures Planning Information by state – www.thearc.org/misc/futplan.html

Dreilinger, D. and Timmons, C. (2001) *From Stress to Success: Making Social Security Work for your Young Adult.* Tools for Inclusion – Institute for Community Inclusion. Available at www.communityinclusion.org

Independent Living Centers are organizations run by and for people with disabilities. Basic services include: information and referral, independent living skills training, peer counseling, and advocacy – www.jik.com/ilcs.html

The National Dissemination Center for Children with disabilities – www.nichcy.org

Social Security Administration – federal office that oversees both Supplemental Security Income and Social Security Disability. Call 1-800-772-1213 to receive information specific to your local community – or go to www.ssa.gov

10

Documentation
and Legal Needs

It is essential that all teenagers have the legal documents that will be required for them to participate in the activities of adult life including but not limited to getting a job, traveling, and cashing a check. An original birth certificate and social security card need to be located and kept in a safe place. Both of these documents will be needed in order for a teenager to obtain paid employment. Teenagers who are not citizens will need to keep their immigration work authorization paperwork up to date.

If the teen does not have a social security card, this is the time to apply for one. Having a social security card is essential for many adult activities including working. If the parent is unable to locate the original social security card, contact the local Social Security Administration[16] office and apply for a new card. Employers are required by law to see the original social security card prior to hiring any new employee. Some families believe that if they know the social security number they do not need the actual card. Just knowing the number is not sufficient in many cases. It is recommended that the social security card be located or obtained as soon as possible.

Students under the age of 18 also need working papers to get a paying job. The guidance office at the teen's school generally issues working papers. The term "working papers" is actually a misnomer. In New York State working papers are actually cards. A blue card is issued if the child is 14 or 15; a green card when the child is 16 or 17. The back of the card contains information regarding the age-related restrictions on hours and types of jobs a student may have. If the teenager is actively seeking employment they should go to the guidance office and initiate the process of applying for working papers. The guidance counselor will need to make a copy of the child's birth certificate and social security card in order to issue working papers. In addition, the teenager must have a current physical on file in the school nurses' office. All teenagers between the ages of 14 and 17 must show an employer their workers' card in order to be hired.

Having a state issued identification card (ID) is essential for all adults. Adults may be required to show ID when traveling, cashing a check, and to obtain employment. If the teenager is not going to get a driver's license in the near future, it is recommended that a parent accompany the teen to the local Department of Motor Vehicles to apply for a non-driver's ID. A non-driver's ID is a state issued picture ID that is accepted as legal identification in the same way as a driver's license. The parent will need to bring their own driver's license and the child's birth certificate and complete the appropriate forms. Even if the teenager hopes to get his driver's license in the future, getting the non-driver ID is a good idea.

Mandated services vs legal accommodations

When a student receiving special education services graduates or ages out of the school system they are no longer eligible for services under the Individuals with Disabilities Education Improvement Act (IDEIA) 2004.[1] IDEIA mandates that every child is entitled to a free and appropriate education and focuses on the development of an Individualized Education Program [3] that includes specialized services that are needed for the child to access an education. It mandates that a results oriented Transition Plan[2] be included in the IEP no later than the year the child is 16. This Transition Plan should address clinical services, housing, financial supports, transportation, medical/insurance needs, employment/post-secondary education, social/personal/recreational opportunities, and legal/advocacy/guardianship needs. All students should be meaningfully involved in the planning process.

IDEIA also requires schools to provide the student who is leaving the school system with a written report that documents the student's academic achievement and functional performance as well as recommendations as to the types of support the student may need to achieve his post-secondary goals. This document is called either a *Student Exit Summary* (SES) or the *Summary of Performance* (SOP). These documents should be given to the student prior to graduation.

IDEIA focuses on the school setting and is applicable only to students who have not yet completed the requirements for a high school diploma, up to the age of 21. Students who do not need a specifically designed educational program to meet their needs may be eligible for special considerations under the Rehabilitation Act or the Americans with Disabilities Act. Latham (2006) summarizes the differences between the Rehabilitation Act, Americans with Disabilities Act (ADA)[19] and IDEIA. She states: "The Rehabilitation Act, most notably Section 504, prohibits discrimination against children and adults with disabilities" (p.1), therefore, providing for accommodations in school and employment. The ADA takes these accommodations further to include private employers with over 15 employees, most private schools, testing entities, and to licensing authorities, regardless of federal funding.

While IDEIA requires the school to develop an IEP that meets the student's needs, the Rehabilitation Act and the ADA are anti-discrimination laws. They provide accommodations for a *qualified* person with a disability throughout his life. In other words a college student must meet all of the eligibility requirements to be accepted to a college program. However, they may request an accommodation if they have a documented disability that warrants this additional service.

The ADA and the Rehabilitation Act do *not* require employers to set aside "special" jobs for people with disabilities. In order to get and keep a job the person must be able to perform the essential functions as defined by the employer. If they choose to disclose the disability they may request a "reasonable accommodation" that will allow them to perform all of the essential functions but they are not entitled to change the written job requirements.

For example, a young adult with a disability who is unable to use a cash register accurately is not eligible for a job in a retail setting that requires use of a cash register as one of the essential functions as per the job description. However, he may be eligible for a job bagging groceries if he has the eye–hand coordination, physical stamina, and ability to stay on task. A "job coach"[6] may be provided as a reasonable accommodation to teach the new worker the specific responsibilities in this work setting. However, the job coach is not supposed to perform the job. The job coach assists the new employee to learn job skills. The adult with a disability is not eligible to be hired for a job if he cannot learn the essential tasks as the employer defines them in a formal written job description.

The job coach does not cost the employer any money and may allow a person with a disability access to a competitive job he might otherwise not be successful at. If he can successfully bag groceries and meet all other essential functions of the job such as to wear a uniform and name tag, speak respectfully to customers, etc. he will continue to have the opportunity to work and be paid at the same rate as any other baggers in that store. Reasonable accommodations are generally no or low cost additions to an employer's budget and remove many of the barriers to employment that could exclude people with disabilities.

Guardianship

Adults with special needs may require additional support and structure to successfully navigate legal issues. Parents are encouraged to explore the ramifications of legal guardianship, as it would impact on the young adult. Legal guardianship gives the named guardian the ability to make legal decisions regarding the child's life after they turn 18 years of age. Some families assume that the child's disability is sufficient to indicate his inability to exercise good judgment and decision-making. Actually, it is the contrary. If an adult's disability impacts on his ability to make complex decisions, affects his judgment, and/or leaves him vulnerable to outside influence, guardianship is recommended as the best way to protect him throughout adult life.

Legal guardianship is a complex matter. Most families seek assistance from an "elder-care" lawyer to explore the pros and cons of guardianship specific to the teen's needs. There are two types of legal guardianship: financial and personal care guardianship. Parents may choose to utilize either or both of these tools depending on the specific challenges of the young adult with special needs.

Financial guardianship will negate the adult with a disability's legal right to make independent financial decisions or enter into a legal contract. This can protect him from being held liable for legal decisions and being taken advantage of by unscrupulous individuals. However, financial guardianship requires the guardian to report annually to the courts on all financial decisions affecting the adult with special needs. This annual report requires stringent bookkeeping and can become burdensome. Families may opt for legal assistance with this aspect of guardianship.

If parents do not set up personal care guardianship, the adult with special needs is legally permitted to make all medical decisions. Parents are not legally entitled to have access to the adult child's confidential medical information unless the young adult gives them written permission. Even school records may not be released to the parent, after the young adult turns 18, unless the young adult gives permission. While medical and school personnel who know the family may not require written permission, if the young adult were to become involved in a legal matter they could be required to stand trial unless legal guardianship has been established.

Families need to weigh the pros and cons of guardianship carefully and the impact it may have on their relationship with the young adult. This process requires the family and the young adult to stand before a judge and state the reasons that guardianship is needed. This can be a painful experience both for the parents and for the adult with special needs who has the ability to understand the process. Again, seeking legal council is recommended, though not necessary to deal most effectively with this complex issue.

Registration for Selective Service

All young men are required to register for Selective Service within 30 days of their eighteenth birthday. Having a disability does not exempt a teenager from Selective Service registration. However, were a draft instituted, the adult's documented disability could preclude them from being required to serve. Draft registration postcards are automatically mailed to the home. If the teenager with special needs does not get a postcard in the mail it can be picked up at the local post office. Registration for selective service can also be done online at www.sss.gov/regver/register-nc.asp.

Selective Service registration is required before a student can be considered for financial aid for college. It is also mandatory for young men who wish to participate in a government work program. Even if the young adult is not planning on pursuing either of those courses, Selective Service registration is required. If the draft was instituted and an adult male is not registered, he may be fined.

Voter registration

One of the adult responsibilities that the young adult with special needs may need assistance with is exercising the right to vote. In the United States, all citizens are eligible to vote once they turn 18 years of age. The young adult with special needs should have some level of familiarity with this process through participation in school elections as well as preparation for voting through the social studies, citizenship, and/or current events curriculum. In many cases, families will need to assist the young adult with the procedures to register to vote as well as to help them sort out the issues and the positions of the candidates. Exercising the right to vote is another opportunity when families can encourage the young adult with special needs to put self-advocacy into action.

Useful resources

Americans with Disabilities Act (ADA) – helpful links include:
   www.ada.gov or www.usdoj.gov

Americans with Disabilities Act Accessibility Guidelines (ADAAG) –
   www.usdoj.gov/crt/ada

Elder-law attorney – www.nelf.org/findcela.asp?

Guardianship – www.expertlaw.com/library

Job Accommodations Network: A service of the Office of Disability Employment Policy of the US Department of Labor –
   www.jan.wvu.edu

League of Women Voters – www.lwv.org

National Center on Educational Outcomes (2006) *What Parents of Students with Disabilities Need to Know and Do.* Available at www.education.umn.edu/nceo

Selective Service Registration – www.sss.gov

Social Security Administration – www.ssa.gov

11

Services and Programs
for Young Adults with
Developmental Disabilities

Office of Developmental Disabilities

The Office of Developmental Disabilities (ODD) in each state is charged with the responsibility of providing essential services for people with a significant cognitive disability, on the autism spectrum, or whose disability limits independence in areas of essential life functions. Determination of eligibility for services through the ODD is based on intelligence testing and/or adaptive life skills scales. These tests can be done by the school psychologist prior to the young adult's aging out of the school system or by a private therapist. They must be updated within one year's time of application for services. Parents may need to contact the young adult's school psychologist and request this update be completed by January of the year the young adult is slated to graduate or exit school. ODD provides services to individuals whose scores fall below a specified level on standardized tests. The school psychologist should be able to guide the family as to the appropriateness of this type of service.

ODD oversees a wide range of adult services and programs. Although programs may vary in different states, the following are programs that will generally operate under the auspices of

ODD: Service Coordination,[13] Day Habilitation, Day Treatment, Supported Employment,[9] various levels of residential support, and recreation programs. This chapter includes a brief description of each of these programs and the types of services they provide. Specific information regarding services in your community can be obtained by contacting the local Developmental Disabilities Service Office.

Service Coordination

Like the mouse of the computer that allows one to navigate the web, a Service Coordinator is the navigator who helps people with special needs and their families to navigate the world of adult services and programs. The Service Coordinator is a trained professional who provides the information and referrals a young adult will need as they transition into adult life. Their primary job is to assess an individual's needs and match them with available programs and services.

Service Coordinators work for adult service agencies. However, their funding is based on Medicaid billing and as such, young adults should have ready access to Service Coordination once they obtain their Medicaid card. Parents can contact the young adult's school counselor/special education coordinator/or the ODD for specific contact information in their community. There are Service Coordinators who can assist a person with a disability to apply for Medicaid. Families may choose to look into this type of Service Coordinator if they require assistance to pursue Medicaid for the young adult who is over 18 years of age.

A Service Coordinator needs to be knowledgeable about the various types of services an adult with special needs may choose, including: eligibility requirements, program offerings, populations served, and availability. With the information provided by the Service Coordinators, families will have the opportunity to take tours of and speak with intake staff from possible programs that will meet the young adult's needs when they exit the school system. Generally it is the responsibility of the Service Coordinator to explain the various programs that a young adult may be eligible for and assist him with the application process. Service Coordinators are an essential link to adult programs and services for people with significant disabilities and as such should be one of the first adult service representatives to join the school's transition team.

Day Habilitation

Day Habilitation (Day Hab) programs are fully supervised settings at which people with disabilities (program participants) are offered opportunities to increase their community participation primarily through volunteer work. Funded by Medicaid, Day Hab programs are designed to provide daily activities for people who meet ODD requirements and who do not work full time. Program participants meet at a central location, referred to as a hub-site. They then organize into small groups and go into the community to perform a variety of community and self-help activities. The activities are selected by the program participants from a menu of choices on a weekly basis.

Some of the biggest advantages of participation in a Day Hab program are: continued opportunities for skill building, opportunities for community participation with supervision as needed, door-to-door transportation, and the flexibility to attend part time and work part time. The focus of Day Hab is to continue skill development to increase the program participant's independence personally, socially, and vocationally. This goal is achieved through participation in unpaid, supervised work experiences and community participation. When the participant demonstrates skills and a level of independence that working requires, they may have the opportunity to move on to paid employment and less restrictive settings. Although some students resist the idea of attending a Day Hab program, most adult program participants report that the program is both enjoyable and interesting and that it provides them with essential outlets for social opportunities.

Day Treatment

Day Treatment programs are in the process of changing over to larger Day Hab programs. These larger programs provide a full array of services designed to meet the needs of people with significant disabilities and/or behavioral challenges. They are designed to assist people who need to limit their community participation to learn the skills that will increase their independence. They are generally located in large buildings with classrooms in which program participants are grouped based on their skills, abilities, needs, and interests. Day Treatment programming is geared towards the development of the skills that prepare a program participant to access the community in a safe and appropriate manner. Day Treatment programs are funded through Medicaid and provide door-to-door transportation as well as an array of clinical services.

Moving out of the family home

For many families, the idea of placing the child even when grown into a residential program smacks of institutionalization. The legacy of institutionalization often continues to overshadow the family's decision when thinking about residential placement. Some families struggle with unresolved personal guilt regarding the child with a disability. Others may have developed a deep-seated distrust for "professionals" who may have appeared to lack understanding of the child with special needs or who may have seemed motivated by their own program's needs rather than by providing quality services. Most families wrestle with concerns regarding the vulnerability of the child or adult with special needs, who depends on the care and assistance of the people around them in order to stay safe and healthy.

In some situations, the family may decide that a professional setting might be better able to provide the amount of structure and support this child or adult needs to continue to grow. Other families feel that it is time for the adult to move from the shelter of his family and experience the independence that supervised living can provide. This decision is always a difficult one. Families must understand that moving an adult into a residential program is not signing them over to the state or an agency and then losing their parental rights. This decision can be reversed at any time the family decides the placement is not meeting the child's or adult's needs. Also, people living in residential programs can and do continue to participate in all of the family activities they did before. Family visits, vacations, and holidays with family are all usual expectations for people living in residences.

Although people with disabilities may lag behind their age peers in their struggle to achieve independence, as they mature, many will eventually wish to separate from their family in more significant ways. Unfortunately, at this time there are many more people waiting for appropriate supported living settings than there are openings. This creates long waiting lists – sometimes as long as ten years! Therefore, it is important for parents to work with the Service Coordinator as soon as possible to complete and submit residential applications to the appropriate adult service agencies. Parents and Service Coordinators will want to identify programs that are consistent with the adult's level of independence. It is recommended that they add the young adult's name to a waiting list even if they are not yet ready to consider this move.

The Service Coordinator should be able to give the family information regarding the various types of residential programs and the populations they serve. Submitting an application does not mean that the family is required to accept an offer but that they will be considered when an appropriate opening becomes available. Completing an application places your child in a "waiting pool" from which appropriate individuals are selected depending on the opening. There will be an interview process that allows the family to learn about the living situation. This process generally follows identification of a possible opening. The interview should also provide agency personnel with essential information about the candidate. Openness during this process will go a long way to ensuring an appropriate match is made between the services available at a particular residence to the applicant's needs. Discussions regarding the person's levels of independence in all skill areas will be essential.

Finding a quality, long-term residential situation is possibly the largest concern many families share when raising a child with a disability. Reliance on other family members for long-term care is often an untenable decision in the long run. Obviously no one will live forever and in the expected course of life most children will outlive their parents. Therefore, setting up long-term residential programming can ensure that the adult with a disability continues to have a safe and healthy lifestyle as long as they live. Although it can be very difficult, families are urged to be proactive in their pursuit of appropriate residential programming while they are still healthy enough to ease the young adult into the new living situation. The most unfortunate situations arise when an adult with a disability is required to move out of their home in crisis, whether it is due to the deterioration of the parents' health, death, or because their own needs have become unmanageable. Long-term planning is the best way to avoid these types of crisis situations.

Currently, there are several different types of living options and residential programs. Each of them is designed to provide a different level of support for the residents in the program. The selection process of matching an individual with a program that can best meet his needs should be carefully considered. Families will want to investigate each of the possible options to determine which will meet the needs of the adult.

Intermediate Care Facilities

Intermediate Care Facilities (ICFs) are designed to provide the most intensive level of supervision and support. Residents may have severe behavioral, medical, and/or cognitive challenges. There will be nursing care provided as needed and staff working in shifts 24 hours a day, seven days a week.

Residents will have opportunities to participate in a variety of activities and to acquire essential skills for adult independence such as grooming, cooking, cleaning, and recreation.

Family Care (sometimes referred to as Adult Foster Care)

A person with special needs may live with a family other than their biological family. The host family receives funds to provide for the essential needs of the person with a disability. Family Care homes are regulated by state and local agencies. The quality of care provided can range from a boarder arrangement to that of a welcomed family member.

Community Residences/Group Homes and Individual Residential Alternatives

Community Residences (CRs) are residential settings in which anywhere from 2 to 12 people with similar support needs live together in a family atmosphere. CRs are staffed 24 hours a day, seven days a week but have less staff than needed in an ICF. Nursing care is usually provided at clinics or day programs, not in the home. People living in CRs attend day programs or hold jobs during the week. There are usually a number of recreational and skill building activities during the evenings and weekends, including but not limited to: cooking, cleaning, self-care, money skills, and community independence training.

Supported Apartments

Supported Apartments (SAs) provide support to people who demonstrate functional levels of independence in personal and homecare but may still need assistance with some of the more complex issues of home and personal management. Staff will be provided for several hours a week to teach and monitor higher level skills such as budgeting, home maintenance, and any safety concerns. Residents of supported apartments most often hold part- or full-time jobs and may also attend part-time day programs. They have also demonstrated a high level of independent participation in the community including the ability to travel either on public transportation or possibly driving their own car.

Home sharing

This arrangement is usually privately set up between a home or apartment owner and a person seeking a room. A roommate may provide assistance and support to the person with a disability or it may be a strictly financial arrangement.

Rent or lease arrangements

People with disabilities may be eligible for subsidized housing through a variety of local housing agencies, service providers, or municipalities. In some areas there are long waiting lists for subsidized apartments. People living in these apartments must be able to see to their own needs. In many cases home health care agencies provide the support that makes this level of independence possible.

Home ownership

The Office of Developmental Disabilities may be able to assist a family to find a mortgage specifically designed for people and families with developmental disabilities. Some families may donate or place a home in a trust fund for the person with special needs to live. Support services may be arranged through home health agencies, an agency serving people with disabilities, a roommate, or the family.

Recreation programs

One way to encourage community experiences and further independence is by seeking out a recreation program that has a specific activity that interests the child/young adult. It is important to apply the same techniques that are successful for other community experiences such as "story boarding"[4] and gradual "fading"[7] of the parent's presence as the child becomes comfortable and enjoys the recreation program. Initially this new experience may require more time, but with support, the child can gradually learn what the expectations are and hopefully begin to enjoy the new program.

A well-designed recreation program offers children and adults with special needs many opportunities for social skills development and community experiences. They provide varying levels of supervision. Parents should expect to provide a clear explanation of the child's disability and the supports he needs to remain safe while participating in the community. Different programs offer varying levels of supervision. Parents need to inquire about the level of support to ensure it matches the child or adult's needs to participate safely and enjoy the program's activities. Some programs offer opportunities for travel both locally and throughout the world.

Recreation programs are often sponsored by adult service agencies, government agencies, community organizations such as the local YMCA, or religious organizations. The cost ranges from nominal through quite expensive. Families need to assess the level of supervision the child needs as well as their interests in order to best determine which program(s) would be best. Recreation programs generally do not provide transportation to the central meeting place. However, transportation to the location of a specific activity is often included. Resources for locating recreation programs are included at the end of this chapter.

Useful resources

The ARC provides programs and advocacy for all children and adults with developmental disabilities – www.thearc.org

The Autism Society of America – www.autism-society.org

The Consortium for Citizens with Disabilities is a coalition of approximately 100 national disability organizations working together to advocate for national public policy that ensures the self-determination, independence, empowerment, integration, and inclusion of children and adults with disabilities in all aspects of society – www.c-c-d.org

Independent Living Centers are organizations run by and for people with disabilities. Basic services include: information and referral, independent living skills training, peer counseling, and advocacy – www.jik.com/ilcs.html

Mental Health Association in Your State – www.nmha.gov

National Mental Health Information Center, Substance Abuse and Mental Health Services Administration (SAMHSA) – www.samhsa.gov

Office of Mental Retardation and Developmental Disabilities – www.omr.state.ny.us

TAC: a non-profit organization that works to achieve positive outcomes on the behalf of people with disabilities and other special needs – www.tacinc.org

12

Services and Programs
for Young Adults
with Mental Health Issues

Office of Mental Health

The Office of Mental Health (OMH) oversees a variety of programs for children and adults with a primary psychiatric diagnosis. These programs are designed to facilitate the development of independent functioning and to provide safe, therapeutic settings for people to work on personal goals. The role of the case management is to oversee a plan of treatment that will facilitate a positive outcome for the person in recovery. Day programs, such as continuing day treatment, clubhouses, and intensive psychiatric rehabilitation and treatment programs, offer educational and therapeutic services depending on the needs of the individual. Residential and recreational programs may also be available.

The fluctuating nature of many psychiatric disorders complicates the process of transition from school to adult services. The teen years are often a time of turmoil, rebellion, and experimentation. While some of this behavior is part of growing up for many young people, teens with a psychiatric illness may experience adolescence in the extreme.

Psychiatric illness is not a developmental disorder, which is to say in many cases psychiatric symptoms may not be present in childhood. It is not unusual for a psychiatric disorder to first manifest itself during the teen years or in later adulthood (17% of all adults worldwide will experience a clinical depression at some point in their lifetime (Comer 2000)). This can make it even more difficult for parents to accept the limitations of this disorder. Having lived with the child prior to the onset of symptoms they may cling to the hope that the symptoms will disappear as the child becomes an adult. There are times when appropriate medications, supportive counseling, and the acquisition of coping skills along with maturity may diminish the impact of the psychiatric symptoms or even completely remove them.

In addition, it is not unusual for people to fear mental illness and the stigma that can accompany it. These emotional concerns may contribute to the lack of funding that is available to provide an appropriate range of services for people with a psychiatric disorder, particularly for young adults who are transitioning from school to adult life. It is often not clear what level of support the young adult with a psychiatric illness needs to manage his illness and meet his potential. The programs that are available generally include people who have a range of symptoms including some with lifelong chronic mental illness, along with people with milder symptoms. It can be very challenging for parents to allow the young adult who is moving out of the school system to participate in an adult program that serves people who exhibit such a wide range of challenges.

Some students are able to meet the requirements for college attendance. Again, families will want to examine closely the quality and depth of support that will be available in this new and more challenging academic setting. Families must have a clear understanding of the academic and social support the teen was receiving in the high school setting, and what the high school program is doing to prepare the young adult for the transition to a post-secondary program. The development of self-advocacy skills should be a major thrust of the high school program and counseling services for the young adult who will be accessing a college program.

The following is a brief list of the types of programs that may be available for people with a primary psychiatric disorder. Families are urged to contact the local Mental Health Services office to ascertain which services will be available for the young adult before they exit the school system. Each of these programs is run by a local mental health agency under the auspices of the state or county Department of Mental Health. Payment for these programs is generally through Medicaid reimbursement or a sliding scale fee system in some cases.

Case managers/service coordinators

The case manager is responsible for overseeing the plan of care that outlines the next steps that will be needed. They will assist the person with psychiatric disabilities and his family to locate and apply for appropriate services. They need to be knowledgeable about types of programs, admission policies, availability, and the populations they serve. Many teens with a psychiatric disability will first encounter the services of a case manager following a hospitalization that was needed in response to a psychiatric behavior problem that could not be managed in the community.

Day programs

While the goal for most adults is to find and maintain competitive employment, people who have chronic psychiatric challenges may have periods when employment is untenable. The Office of Mental Health offers the following programs that are designed to provide ongoing training and support. These programs can offer structured environments as well as an avenue for skill development, social, and recreational outlets.

Continuing Day Treatment program

Continuing Day Treatment (CDT) programs are the most structured of OMH outpatient programs. They help individuals who are in need of assistance to develop positive coping mechanisms with daily activities designed to address the individual needs of the participant. Programs address activities of daily living and/or socialization skills development as needed by the individual. Attendance in this program is considered long term. Transportation may be available for some program participants.

Psychosocial clubs – club houses

Club houses are central meeting places that offer services for people with psychiatric disabilities. There are generally opportunities for socialization, recreation, and pre-vocational training. Each program varies depending upon the needs and interests of the program participants. Participants may choose to focus on the development of pre-vocational skills and training and/or positive work behaviors in a supportive environment. There is no cost to the program participant but transportation must be arranged on an individual basis.

Intensive Psychiatric Rehabilitation and Treatment programs

Intensive Psychiatric Rehabilitation and Treatment programs (IPRTs) offer people a range of courses that are time limited and focus on specific skills and topics. Course selection is made by the program participant with the assistance of their in-house counselor and is based on the participant's desire to make positive changes in his life. Some examples of courses that may be offered at an IPRT program are resumé preparation, interview skills, computer desktop skills, managing personal behaviors, etc. People choose which courses they wish to sign up for and are encouraged to attend each session. Arrangements for transportation to and from these programs are individually determined. IPRTs are Medicaid funded programs but sliding scale fees can be arranged if needed.

Useful resources

Community Resources Database of Long Island (2006) *Transitioning to Adulthood: A Resource List to Help Youth with Behavioral Health Disorders Transition to Adulthood.* Available at www.crdli.org

Independent Living Centers – organizations run by and for people with disabilities. Basic services include: information and referral, independent living skills training, peer counseling, and advocacy – www.jik.com/ilcs.html

Mental Health Association in your state – www.nmha.gov

National Mental Health Information Center, Substance Abuse and Mental Health Services Administration (SAMHSA) – www.samhsa.gov

State Mental Health Services, a list by state to reach local services – www.cdc.gov/mentalhealth/state/orgs.htm

WebMD, for online information and advice about depression – www.webmd.com/depression

Chapter 13

Employment

The eventual goal for most people when they leave school whether from a special education program or an Ivy League college is to find a job. Although many adults with special needs will continue to require financial support from government sources, having employment increases personal income. But perhaps even more important, employment is an avenue that provides meaningful use of time, gives structure to daily activities, builds personal confidence, and allows for social outlets. The development of job skills and the identification of vocational interests should be a major thrust of the special education student's Transition Plan[2] during their last few years in school where appropriate. It should not be a mystery as to the type of work and/or skills the student still needs to master in order for him to work following graduation. Participation in paid and/or unpaid work is the best way to identify vocational aptitudes, strengths, and interests.

Optimally, a student's job interests and skills can be targeted to align with job availability in his community. Unfortunately, there are times when this is not the case. The student may look into additional training or education or he may decide to work in a less preferred job and continue to pursue his dream as a hobby.

The need for appropriate social skills and demeanor cannot be overemphasized as a deal maker or breaker in employment.

Employers can train people to do the skills needed for a particular job, but they cannot train them to fit into the culture of the workplace. Skills such as dressing appropriately for the job setting, flexibility, problem-solving, organization, and following the "unwritten rules" of a particular workplace are invaluable. A good worker arrives at work reliably and on time. He demonstrates appropriate social demeanor in dealing with supervisors, co-workers, and customers. Parents, schools, and work programs must teach these skills and behaviors as they are essential for finding and maintaining employment. Adults who have acquired appropriate social skills find it easier to get and to keep a job regardless of their disability.

Vocational Rehabilitation Services
(In New York State – Vocational and Education Services for Individuals with Disabilities)

Adults with a documented disability who want to work are eligible to meet with the state vocational rehabilitation counselor to discuss employment options. Vocational rehabilitation services may be available to people who do not qualify for Social Security benefits, Office of Developmental Disabilities (ODD) or Office of Mental Health (OMH) programs. It can be helpful to meet with a vocational rehabilitation counselor one to two years prior to the anticipated date of graduation in order to determine eligibility and explore relevant support options.

Vocational Rehabilitation Services may provide assistance finding a job, job coaching,[6] job training, and possibly even financial assistance for vocationally related coursework. The type of support will be determined by the vocational rehabilitation counselor after reviewing the young adult's academic, psychological, and medical records and discussing with the young adult their vocational interests and limitations. The young adult needs to be prepared to discuss his disability and how it specifically impacts on his ability to work. It is recommended that the family and the counselor, when available, prepare the young adult for this meeting by helping him to describe his challenges in functional language.

Commission for the Blind and Visually Handicapped

Commission for the Blind and Visually Handicapped (CBVH) provides vocational and life skills services to people who are legally blind. CBVH assistance is not strictly limited to vocationally oriented programming. Parents may wish to contact this agency to determine whether or not the child meets the eligibility requirements. Specific contact information is listed at the end of this chapter.

Supported Employment

One of the options that may be available through vocational rehabilitation services is Supported Employment.[9] Supported Employment is a program that provides hands-on, on-the-job training. It is designed for people who do not generalize information well and therefore will learn best from real life experience. Job coaches are trained staff who provide the support that is needed for a person with a disability to learn job skills. Job coaches may also assist with job development i.e. finding an available position that is related to the person's skills. The job coach may accompany the job applicant through the entire hiring process and then provide essential support and assistance as needed on the job.

The job coach does not only teach the skills needed to do the job but will also help the new worker to understand the culture and social expectations of the workplace and the skills needed to integrate into that culture. They will, when necessary, educate co-workers as to the types of assistance the new employee may need and in the process identify a "natural support" co-worker[8] who can be a go-to person for the beginning worker. Gradually the job coach "fades"[7] from the job as the new worker demonstrates competence and awareness of the social requirements.

Initially, job coaches are directly involved in the daily completion of all job tasks. However, over time, the worker should be able to perform all required work skills, allowing the coach to fade while the job continues. Supported Employment is based on competitive employment. This means the worker is paid the competitive rate and must therefore meet all of the essential functions of the job such as joining the union, when available; multi-tasking when requested; dressing appropriately; and any of the requirements that other employees must meet.

It is essential that an adult who is seeking employment, even with the assistance of a supported employment program, has community-based safety skills and has demonstrated independence in a variety of community settings. A student who is unable to access local businesses independently and appropriately would not be a candidate for employment until they are able to demonstrate these skills.

Reasonable accommodation

Although the Americans with Disabilities Act (1990) (ADA)[19] protects individuals with documented disabilities, it states in Section 12.1118 that the employee must be able to perform all "essential functions"[20] of a job as defined by the employer. In order to seek protection under the ADA, the worker must reveal the nature of his disability to the employer. If needed, the worker may request appropriate accommodations that will allow him to meet the job requirements. It is recommended that a potential employee not discuss his disability until he has officially been hired. In fact, employers prefer not to be made aware of a person's disability prior to hiring, as this knowledge can leave the employer open to legal repercussions if they choose not to hire this person for whatever reason.

The use of a job coach is an accommodation that employers are generally told about prior to hiring. In this case, the job developer who is looking for a job will need to exercise caution in presenting the potential employee's ability. Discussing an applicant's disability is counterproductive and illegal, unless the job applicant has given his permission. Employers are much more likely to offer a job to someone whom they perceive as being able to do the job, as opposed to hiring someone whose disability has been the focus of the interview. Therefore, job developers need to focus on the skills the applicant will bring to the job and the support services that will allow him to meet all of the employer's requirements.

Further reading and useful resources

American Foundation for the Blind lists information in the US and Canada that provide services to people who are blind – www.afb.org/services.asp

Commission for the Blind and Visually Handicapped – services for New York State – www.ocfs.state.ny.us/main

Grandin, T. and Duffy, K. (2004) *Developing Talents: Careers for Individuals with Asperger Syndrome and High-Functioning Autism.* Shawnee Missions, KS: Autism Asperger Publishing.

Griffin, G. and Hammis, D. (2003) *Making Self-Employment Work for People with Disabilities.* Baltimore, MD: Paul T. Brookes Publishing Co.

Job Accommodation Network – www.jan.wvu.edu

Okahashi, P. (2001) "Influencing self-employment success for people with developmental disabilities." *Rehabilitative Review 12,* 5. Available at www.vrri.org/content/view/141/120

Okahashi, P. (2001) "Self-employment for people with developmental disabilities." *Rehabilitative Review 12,* 4, 75–85.

"Supported self employment: A guide to assisting individuals with developmental disabilities" – www.ddpc.state.ny.us

In Closing...

The purpose of this book is to provide families with information and referral sources so they can effectively advocate with their child and plan together for his future. Families will want to use the resources at the end of each chapter to gain more information about topics of special interest to them. With this information they can make informed choices about opportunities that will impact on the child throughout his life.

While much of the available information about people with special needs focuses on a specific type of disability, parents would be wise to disregard the specific disability label and review information that includes topics or areas of interest to them. They will most likely find that much of the information is relevant to people with a wide range of disabling conditions. For example, although people on the autism spectrum can be characterized as requiring social expectations broken down for them, the same may be true for people with many different challenges. Therefore, a book that is written about teaching social skills to people with autism could be useful to parents of children with many other types of disabilities as well.

Perhaps the best gift a parent can give the adult with a disability is an understanding of his unique challenges and the specific tools he can use to compensate for those challenges to the best of his ability. Optimally, the person with special needs will be able to describe the types of support that allow him to live and work as independently as he is able. He must ask for the accommodations he needs to participate in his community of choice. Information regarding his special needs must be in language that he and other people can understand. Whenever possible he needs to identify and explain the essential supports that will allow him to participate successfully in community life and/or post-secondary training opportunities including higher education. I wish each and every family the courage to give this gift to their child as they head out into the world.

Notes

1. Cortiella (2006) summarizes and compares two federal laws: the *No Child Left Behind Act* and the *Individuals with Disabilities Education Act* (IDEA). The study states that the IDEA requires that "the education provided to children with disabilities must meet the unique needs resulting from the child's disability and must enable the child to be involved and make progress in the general education curriculum." (p.9) The IDEA is a law designed to ensure that local schools serve the educational needs of students with disabilities. The updated IDEIA of 2004 requires that all states that accept IDEA funds provide a "free and appropriate" public education to all children with disabilities. Every state is required to:

    *   set a goal of providing full educational opportunity to all children with disabilities and a timetable for accomplishing that goal
    *   identify, locate and evaluate all children with disabilities who are in need of special education services
    *   ensure that all special education teachers are highly qualified
    *   evaluate every child suspected of having a disability
    *   develop an annual IEP for each child with a disability
    *   provide education services in the least restrictive environment
    *   provide all procedural safeguards as outlined by IDEA
    *   establish goals for the performance of children with disabilities that are consistent with standards for all children in that state
    *   include all children with disabilities in general state and district wide assessment programs.

    (p.8–9)

IDEA does not "hold schools accountable for the progress and performance of children with disabilities." The "NCLB requires all states to have challenging academic content standards…" (p.9)

2. The IDEA requires a Transition Plan be included in each student's IEP the year he turns 16 or earlier. The Rhode Island Parent Information Network (2005) defines transition planning as "a means for setting goals, planning and preparing for life after high school, making sure that the student's high school experience gives him or her the skills, connections, and experiences to succeed after high school." (p.1) The IDEA, Section 300.18 requires the Transition Plan to be a coordinated set of activities for a student, designed within an outcome-oriented process, that promotes movement from school to post-school activities, including post-secondary education, vocational training, integrated employment (including Supported Employment), continuing and adult education, adult services, independent living, and community participation. The "coordinated set of activities" must be based on the individual student's needs, taking into account the student's preferences and interests, and include instruction, community experiences, the development of employment and other post-school living objectives, and where appropriate, the acquisition of daily living skills.

3. Individualized Education Program (IEP) is a document that outlines the educational program of a student who is identified in need of special educational services. While the format may vary in different states, it must include clear and useful information specifying the student's:

    - current level of performance
    - annual goals (benchmarks) including how they will be measured and levels of mastery
    - related services
    - extent to which the child will not participate in regular educational classes and other school activities
    - extent to which the child will participate in state and district-wide tests

- date services will begin, how often they will be provided, where they will be provided, and how long they will last

- how parents will be informed of progress.

4. "Story boarding" – a technique commonly used in the field of visual arts in which a series of pictures is presented sequentially to show the steps of a process or social behavior. Photographs, line drawings, and/or key words are laid out on to separate pieces of paper or across a large board in sequence. People who are visual learners may find this a useful tool when preparing for an upcoming event, learning the steps of a new activity, or to acquire new information.

5. Hoekman (2006) details this Social Stories™ technique developed and trademarked by Carol Gray that follows the Social Stories™ guidelines and criteria found in Social Stories™ 10.0. The goal of a Social Story™ is to recognize achievements or to share accurate social information in a patient and reassuring manner that is easily understood by its audience.

6. Job coach – accompanies a person with a disability to his job and helps him to learn the job requirements and the skills he needs to integrate into a work setting. Job coaches may also assess a person's job aptitudes and skills, locate an appropriate job, travel train, and set up routines regarding job responsibilities. Job coaching is usually a time limited support service funded through vocational rehabilitation services programs.

7. Fading is a gradual decrease in guidance and support based on the acquisition of new skills. Job coaches in supported employment settings rely on fading techniques to facilitate the learning of work skills.

8. Natural support – a co-worker or peer who serves as the go-to person and informally sees that the person with a disability receives and understands information that will help them to fit in.

9. Supported Employment – a reasonable accommodation under the ADA in which an employee with special needs is provided with a job coach paid for by a rehabilitation agency in an integrated and competitive job.

10. Reader – a reasonable accommodation under the Rehabilitation Act of 1975. A staff member or volunteer who reads aloud material or test information for a person with a documented disability that limits his processing of visual information or who is legally blind.

11. Person Centered Planning (PCP) – a technique designed to gather information based on a person's interests, aptitudes, abilities, and support needs. This information is then put into a plan of action with clearly defined roles and a timeframe for completion. Also referred to as Personal Futures Planning or MAPs. A PCP should include the people who work closely with the individual as well as any close family members or friends who have a stake in the individual's future dreams and plans.

12. Individual Educational Program (IEP) or Committee on Special Education (CSE) meeting. As per IDEA mandate, this meeting must include the parent or designated legal guardian or representative, specific members of the educational team, and the student where appropriate. One team member can serve dual roles if qualified and parents may give written permission to hold the meeting without a particular representative. The team meets one time per school year or more as needed to determine whether or not special education services are needed and to write and/or review the IEP including goals and support services for the next school year.

13. Service Coordinators – provide relevant information to people with disabilities and their families regarding support services to meet their needs. Service coordinators work for an adult service agency under the auspices of the Office of Developmental Disabilities or the Department of Mental Health.

14. General Education Diploma (GED) – an alternative method for obtaining a high school diploma for students who no longer attend regular high school.

15. 504 Plan – a written plan updated annually that provides for students with disabilities who only require reasonable accommodations.

16. Social Security Administration – federal government program that provides monthly income to people who are disabled, workers who become disabled and their families as well as people who retire.

17. Supplemental Needs Trust – irrevocable trust created for people with a disability to pay for non-essential expenses not covered by government support programs.

18. Substantial Gainful Employment (SGA) – Social Security's guideline for determining whether a disability impacts on employability, if the disability impedes the person from becoming self-supporting and attaining SGA.

19. Americans with Disabilities Act (ADA) – a federal law protecting the rights of individuals with disabilities. www.ada.gov

20. US Department of Justice (1990) Section 12111.8 Essential Functions – "Essential functions are the basic job duties that an employee must be able to perform, with or without reasonable accommodation."

References

Baker, B. and Brithman, A. (1997) *Steps to Independence: Teaching Everyday Skills to Children with Special Needs.* Baltimore, MD: Paul H. Brookes Publishing Co.

Comer, R.J. (2000) *Abnormal Psychology.* New York: Worth Publishers.

Cortiella, C. (2006) *NCLB and IDEA: What Parents of Students with Disabilities Need to Know and Do.* Minneapolis, MN: National Center on Educational Outcomes, University of Minnesota. Available in pdf form at www.education.umn.edu/NCEO/OnlinePubs/Parents.pdf – accessed 16 July 2007.

Hoekman, L. (2006) *Balancing the Social Equation Using Social Stories™ and Social Articles.* Kentwood, MI: The Gray Center for Social Learning and Understanding. Available at www.thegraycenter.org/store/index.cfm?fuseaction=page.display&page_id=74&CFID= 902200&CFTOKEN= 10829367 – accessed 22 February 2007.

Hughes, C. and Carter, E. (2000) *The Transition Handbook: Strategies High School Teachers Use that Work!* Baltimore, MD: Paul H. Brookes Publishing Co.

IDIEA (2004) *Building the Legacy: IDEA 2004.* Washington, DC: US Department of Education. Available at http://idea.ed.gov – accessed 2 September 2007.

Latham, P. (2006) *The Law After High School.* LD online, WETA. Available at www.Idonline.org/article/6098 – accessed 16 July 2007.

National Center on Secondary Education and Transition and PACER Centre (2004) *Parent Brief – Person-Centered Planning: A Tool for Transition.* Available at www.ncset.org/publications/viewdesc.asp?id=1431 – accessed 16 July 2007.

New York State Developmental Disabilities Planning Council (2006) *Planning for the Future: A Guide for Families and Friends of People with Developmental Disabilities.* Available at www.ddpc.state.ny.us – accessed 17 July 2007.

Pataki, G. (2006) *Planning for the Future: A Guide for Families and Friends of People with Developmental Disabilities, 6th edition.* New York State Developmental Disabilities Planning Council. Available at www.ddpc.state.ny.us/publications/education/version6.pdf

Rhode Island Parent Information Network (2005) *Here's to Your Student's Future! A Parent's Guide to Transition Planning.* Available at www.ripin.org/transitionguideeng.pdf – accessed 16 July 2007.

Rubin, B.M. and Aduroja, G. (2005) "Down Syndrome Barriers Falling with New College-degree Opportunities." *The Chicago Tribune,* 12 December.

US Department of Justice (1990) *Americans with Disabilities Act,* Section 12111.8. Available at www.ada.gov/pubs/ada.htm – accessed July 2007.

Wehman, P. (2006) *Life Beyond the Classroom – Transition Strategies for Young People with Disabilities.* Baltimore, MD: Paul H. Brookes Publishing Co.

WNY Collegiate Consortium of Disability Advocates (2006) *Effective College Planning, 9th Edition.* Available at www.ccdanet.org/ecp – accessed 17 July 2007.

Index

Rosie and Prunella
spent the day delivering valentines.
They were happy to be friends again.
And Prunella looked terrific
wearing her new sardine.

"Gee, thanks, Prunella,"
said Rosie.
"It's the nicest
valentine I ever got."

"This is for you, Rosie,"
Prunella said.

She handed Rosie a big red heart
trimmed with lace.
It smelled like perfume,
and it read:

ROSES ARE RED.
VIOLETS ARE BLUE.
VALENTINE'S DAY
IS NO FUN WITHOUT YOU!

Rosie held her nose
and carried the valentine
to Prunella's house.
Prunella was just coming out the door.

Then she wrote:

"I'll surprise her,"
thought Rosie.
"I'll make her the meanest, greenest
valentine I can."

Rosie made a big green heart.
She messed it up with bug juice.

"At least she let me blow them out first,"
Rosie thought.
All of a sudden,
she missed Prunella.
Prunella was fun even if she was awful.
Rosie thought of the valentines
Prunella had made.
So what if they were slimy?
Prunella had worked hard on them.

There was the time she
ate the candles on Rosie's birthday cake.

Rosie was still mad at Prunella.
She remembered all the bad things
Prunella had ever done.
There was the time
she put fleas in Rosie's pajamas.

Prunella felt awful.

She really missed Rosie.

But no matter what she did,

Rosie would not come out and play.

But Prunella wouldn't give up.
Her next valentine said,

"Ouch! Ouch!" yelled Rosie.
"Go away!"

"Pee-yew!" said Rosie
and threw the valentine out.
"Get lost!" she yelled.

Then she wrote:

"Rosie *has* to like this one,"
thought Prunella.

"What's not to like?"
wondered Prunella.
She went home and tried again.
She made a big heart
and dipped it in skunk juice.

"Achoo! Achoo!"
sneezed Rosie from inside.
"I don't like that valentine!"

Prunella sprinkled sneezing powder
on the valentine and
went to Rosie's house.
She put the valentine
under the door and waited.

"This is the best valentine ever.
Rosie's going to love it!" thought Prunella.
The valentine read:

OH, HOW I LOVE
YOUR MONSTER SMILE.
YOU LOOK JUST LIKE
A CROCODILE!

"I'll make her a valentine,"
thought Prunella.
"Then she won't be mad anymore."

Prunella made Rosie a giant gray heart
with sickly purple trim.

She remembered how Rosie had
let her get a head start
in the Monster Marathon.

Prunella started to miss Rosie.

"Who else should I make a valentine for?"
wondered Prunella.
Rosie was the only one she could think of.
She remembered all the times
she had broken things
and Rosie had fixed them.

She made one for her dentist:

Prunella went home
and made a valentine for her uncle.
It read:

DEAR UNCLE NED,
GO SOAK YOUR HEAD!

TOAD
JAM

Prunella hummed as she worked,
and she really put a lot of slime
on that valentine.

"Fine!" said Prunella.

"I will make my own valentines.

I have plenty of slime at home."

"Good," said Rosie.

"Who wants slime anyway?"

Rosie stamped her foot.
"At my house
you can only make nice valentines,"
said Rosie.

"No, they're not.
They are mean and green!"
said Rosie.

"That's what makes them so great,"
said Prunella.

"Don't you have any green slime
to put on the valentines?"
Prunella asked Rosie.

Rosie was really upset.
She said,
"Prunella, valentines
are supposed to be *nice*!"

"Mine *are* nice!"
said Prunella.

And she made an extra-fancy one
for her parents:

She made one for the letter carrier:

"But valentines aren't supposed
to be *mean!*" said Rosie.

Prunella didn't listen.
She was busy making a valentine
for her neighbor:

ROSES ARE RED.
VIOLETS ARE BLUE.
I THINK All TEACHERS
BELONG IN THE ZOO.

Prunella held it up proudly.
"You're right, Rosie,"
she said. "Valentines are fun!"

"Oh, all right," said Prunella.

"I'll make one for my karate teacher."

Prunella took a piece of
icky green paper.
She tore it into
the shape of a heart.
She found some dust under Rosie's bed.
She sprinkled it on the heart.
Then she wrote the message.

Rosie held up a pink valentine.
It read:

Roses are red.
Violets are blue.
Cupcakes are sweet
And so are you.

"Try making one," said Rosie.

"What should we do today?"
asked Prunella.

"It's Valentine's Day,"
said Rosie.
"Let's make valentines."

"I hate making valentines!"
said Prunella.

"But it's *fun*," said Rosie.
"Look at this one.
It's for my piano teacher."

Prunella ate some more of the bed.
"There, now it doesn't wobble anymore,"
she said.

"You think of everything, Prunella,"
said Rosie politely.

Prunella's idea of being nice to Rosie
was to eat part of her bed.

"My bed always wobbles
after you come over,"
complained Rosie.

"I am starting a stamp collection, too,"
said Prunella.

"Really?" said Rosie.

"Yes," said Prunella.
"Here is the first stamp."

And she stamped very hard on Rosie's foot.

"Ouch!" said Rosie.

One winter day Prunella came over
to Rosie's house.
Rosie was working on her stamp collection.
"I have hundreds of stamps from
all over the world," she said.

Twing.
twing.
twing.

Prunella liked to howl at the moon.
She liked to *eat* flowers and mud pies.

Even though Rosie and Prunella
were so different,
they still liked each other.

Rosie liked to sing songs.
She liked to pick flowers
and make mud pies.

But Rosie was nice.
She was not like other monsters.

Prunella was mean —
the way monsters
are supposed to be.

Rosie and Prunella were best friends.

To Phil,
my one and only Valentine
                    —J.C.

To my daughters, Jana and Jennifer,
who posed for Prunella and Rosie.
                    —J.L.

ISBN 0-590-42216-2

Text Copyright © 1990 by Joanna Cole.
Illustrations copyright © 1990 by Jared D. Lee Studio, Inc.
All rights reserved. Published by Scholastic Inc.

12 11 10 9 8 7 6 5 4 3 2 1   0 1 2 3 4 5/9

Printed in the U.S.A.   11

First Scholastic printing, January 1990

MONSTER VALENTINES

by JOANNA COLE

pictures by JARED LEE

SCHOLASTIC INC.

New York Toronto London Auckland Sydney